Young Pathfinder 10

A CILT series for primary language teachers

A world of languages

Developing children's love of languages

Manjula Datta and Cathy Pomphrey

CiLT The National Centre for Languages

The views expressed in this publication are the authors' and do not necessarily represent those of CILT.

Acknowledgements

The authors would like to thank Jessica, Nirmala, Namita, Tom, Nitya, Parul, Leonidas, Sebastian, Yuki and Lisa for their contributions to the ideas included in the book. A special thanks to the parents of these children for allowing us to talk to them and for supporting our work with examples.

Thanks also to our student teachers who have contributed to the book by trying out different approaches to language teaching and language awareness work in the classroom over many years.

We are grateful to Oliver Cunningham and David McGonaghie for supplying the graphic representation of a language autobiography of Tanya Datta.

Many of our colleagues have supported our work and supplied relevant material; we are grateful to them for this. Alan Smith has provided invaluable support with much of the visual material. We would also like to mention the support of: Tozun Issa, Mrs Pembe Issa, Redouane Aghouyai, Suresh Jethwa, David Cross, Julie Adams, Mohamed Guenuni, Tereza Trantinova, Maria Neophytou and Kalpana Agrawal. Finally, we would like to thank Emma Rees at CILT for her continuous encouragement.

First published 2004 by CILT, the National Centre for Languages, WC2N 4LB.

Copyright © CILT 2004
Illustrations by Richard Duszczak

Cover photography © Barbara Ludman/iwitness 2003

ISBN 1 904243 20 7

Cover design by Neil Alexander

Printed in Great Britain by Hobbs

CILT Publications are available from: **Central Books**, 99 Wallis Rd, London E9 5LN. Tel: 0845 458 9910. Fax: 0845 458 9912. Book trade representation (UK and Ireland): **Broadcast Book Services**, Charter House, 29a London Rd, Croydon CR0 2RE. Tel: 020 8681 8949. Fax: 020 8688 0615.

Contents

Ackowledgements

The authors and publisher would like to acknowledge the following for permission to reproduce copyright material: p10: *Words for school* (Mantra Publishing Ltd); p10 *Mathaino chromatizontas* by Beta Blust, Edition Graphic Arts, M Vasilakis, E Triperinas & Sia C.O.; pp13, 19 & 53 photos by Barbara Ludman © 2000, 2003, 2000; p25: *Chinese Cinderella* by Adeline Yen Mah (Pearson Education Ltd); p27: *A balloon for Grandad* (original English version) by Nigel Gray and Jane Ray (Orchard Books); p28: *Muhamad's desert night* by Cristina Kessler (Puffin Books); p30: 'The boogey man's wife' by V Aardema and R Ruffins from *Misoso once upon a time tales from Africa* (Penguin); p33: *Farmer duck* (Vietnamese and English) by Martin Waddell and Helen Oxenbury (Magi Publications); pp37 and 54: 'The journey of ginger map' and Chinese characters from *World languages project* by Sol Garson et al (Hodder & Stoughton, 1989) reproduced by permission of Hodder Arnold; pp44–45: *We're going on a bear hunt* by Michael Rosen and Helen Oxenbury (Walker Books, 1989); pp45 & 47: *Handa's surprise* by Eileen Browne (Walker Books, 1994); p47: 'Ríkadlo pro lidoopy' from *Pro slepičí kvoč* by Jiří áček (Albatros); p48: 'Sluníčko Sedmitečné' by František Hrubín and A Zábranský from *Je nám dobře na světě* (Státní nakladatelství dětské knihy); p54: *The swirling Hijaab* (Urdu and English) by Na'ima bint Robert and Nilesh Mistry, *Pandora's box* (Vietnamese and English) by Henriette Barkow and Diana Mayo (Mantra Publishing Ltd), *Don't cry, Sly!* (Panjabi and English) by Henriette Barkow and Richard Johnson; pp55–56: *Bengali alphabet chart* from Portsmouth Ethnic Minority Achievement Service; p56: Bulus Turkish delight and Ülker deluxe wafers; p59: 'Nicht nur popcorn' from *Kinder* magazine (1993: 4); p65: 'Micky always' from *I din do nuttin and other poems* by John Agard (Bodley Head).

In some cases it has not been possible to trace copyright holders of material reproduced in this book. The publisher will be pleased to make the appropriate arrangement with any copyright holder whom it has not been possible to contact at the earliest opportunity.

Introduction

A world of languages is written for teacher colleagues and trainee teachers working with primary age children. It aims to help them develop children's love of languages by providing stimulating activities which raise awareness and enjoyment of the languages of the world. We believe that a multilingual approach to language development helps to deepen children's understanding of what language is, how it works and how it is used in different contexts, which in turn strengthens the teaching and learning objectives of the National Literacy Strategy at text, word and sentence level. The examples used in the book include and recognise the linguistic diversity of people in Britain. They enable teachers to acknowledge and use in classroom learning the languages of children who are bilingual, enabling these children to develop the self-esteem and confidence in their own language knowledge necessary to learn and understand language at a deep level. When children's language learning extends beyond English into other languages, it not only provides the stimulus to learn a new language but also allows them to think about language more deeply and flexibly. Children who are native speakers of English will also have much to contribute to the teaching approaches advocated here, as the children's voices in the first chapter clearly demonstrate. Children learn about languages through sharing and observing the language behaviours all around them in our multicultural society, even if they are speakers of only one language. Monolingual teachers, working together with bilingual teachers or adults, or on their own, through some of the suggested activities can provide meaningful language learning experiences for the children in their classes. This is especially important in parts of the country where there is less diversity as it enables children in these contexts to access some of the advantages which a multilingual environment provides in enriching understanding of what language is and how it works. In Chapter 2 we look specifically at ways that teachers can work together with bilingual adults to bring other languages into the classroom.

Many of the ideas included in the book come from our own experience of working with young learners in multilingual classrooms. The book shows how teachers can raise linguistic and cultural awareness by providing opportunities to talk and engaging children in language learning activities. The main resource for learning is children's languages, and this includes English. We believe that multiculturalism is not just about 'other' cultures, but about getting to know our own language and culture through collaborative talk and activities. Children have a special way with words, as the children who helped us with the book demonstrate.

Throughout the book teachers will find ideas for interactive language activities, which celebrate diversity and allow children to articulate, share and extend their knowledge of many aspects of language and culture (their metalinguistic and sociolinguistic knowledge). We hope that teachers will enjoy using these activities and will build on them with their own ideas and those of the children in their classes. The following quote conveys the principle of inclusion on which this book is based.

> *The curriculum that is taught in schools needs to incorporate each individual child's background, to give them self-worth and for them to have pride in who they are.*
> (Doreen Lawrence 1999)

1. Personal language diversity – you know more than you think

This chapter aims to:

- raise children's awareness of linguistic and cultural diversity among individual pupils and in society through talk;

- give examples of children's voices showing their knowledge about language:
  - at a metalinguistic level, for example, their ability to stand outside language and talk about languages and language varieties;
  - at a sociolinguistic level, for example, how language uses vary in different social contexts, i.e. from spoken to standard, regional and dialectal varieties, bilingual switches between languages and language varieties;
  - their understanding of language acquisition processes;
  - their understanding of the inextricable relationship between language and culture;

- suggest supportive interactive activities, which celebrate diversity and encourage children to reflect on their personal experiences and observations and develop interest in learning another language.

CHILDREN'S AWARENESS OF DIVERSITY

When given the opportunity, children love to talk about language. We often underestimate how much they know. Even very young children can already have significant knowledge about language, as you can see from the example of three year-old Nitya among the children's voices below.

Most children have some experience of linguistic and cultural diversity in their lives. This may be because family members or friends use different languages or speak English with different accents, use a different variety of English or use dialect words or phrases. They may hear different accents or different languages on television or when away from home on holiday. Children sometimes have friends or members of the family living abroad or in different parts of the UK. Sometimes they hear people using different languages or different varieties of English in the neighbourhood, on the street or in shops.

The awareness that language is used differently by different people in different contexts is an important step in the process of standing back from language use in order to compare, categorise and conceptualise language forms and structures. This may also create an interest in learning new languages. Children who are bilingual have an advantage in this. Because they conduct their lives in more than one language, different language uses are part of their immediate and everyday experience. However they still need support in articulating and sharing their knowledge to make it more explicit. Those who do not have the advantage of living in more than one language on an everyday basis need other stimuli to help them talk about language and languages, as suggested in this chapter and throughout the book. The examples and activities described below show how teachers could bring different voices and examples of a wide variety of language uses into the classroom.

CHILDREN'S VOICES ON THEIR LANGUAGE USES

The young people in the examples below, Nitya, Jessica, Tom, Nirmala and Namita, reveal a deep knowledge about language, albeit implicit, when asked to talk about their experiences and perceptions of how people use language.

Nitya, a fluent Hindi speaker, arrived in England when she was three. When exposed to English in her nursery school she made some insightful comments, which indicate the thinking processes of a bilingual relating to a new social context and its corresponding language use. After three weeks in the nursery, talking to her father she remarked in Hindi:

> *'Papa, hum nursery mei English boltei hain.'* (Papa, we speak in English in the nursery.)
> *'Aur hum ghur mei Hindi boltei hain, leikin hum English bhi boltei hain'*. (And at home we speak in Hindi but we speak in English as well.)

Another example shows her developing knowledge about language as a result of operating between two languages:

> *'Tota maney* [means] *parrot, bandar maney monkey, baagh maney tiger, shaer maney lion, cheetah maney … Papa, what's the English word for cheetah?'* she asked her father in Hindi.

Readers may know that *'cheetah'* was a loan word from Indian languages and is now absorbed into English. In her dialogue Nitya is pairing the names of animals in Hindi and English and mentally forming linguistic structural patterns in her mind as she explores the relationship between her two languages. Young and new language learners very often engage in such linguistic pattern making. Because she is in contact with two languages, she is already in a position to understand a very complex linguistic and philosophical concept, the way in which the name of something in any language can be separated from the object it represents. She is also ready to understand how languages link and borrow from each other. (See Chapter 6 'What is English?' for further exploration of language links.)

Yuen Ren Chao, an American linguist, said:

> *'Monolingual persons take language so much for granted that they often forget its arbitrary nature and cannot distinguish words from things.'*
> (Yuen Ren Chao 1968)

Jessica, an eight year-old native English speaker from North London, demonstrates interesting insights into how people use and learn language from her experience and observations:

Q: Do you know what other languages children in your class speak?

J: *There are Russian people, Iranian people, African people, American and Asian people in my class ...*

Obviously, for Jessica, languages are associated with people; she understands that there are links between identity and language use.

Q: Do they speak English like you?

J: *Most of them* [do but] *some don't because their first language isn't English.* [On further questioning Jessica said some of her classmates had arrived recently in London].

Q: Suppose you saw two Russian girls talking in their language, would you be able to guess what they're talking about?

J: *No ...* [engrossed in thinking]

Q: What about their way of speaking?

J: *Yes ... if they're angry their voices will be quite loud ... if they're talking about happy things they'll be laughing, if they're talking about sad things they'll be saying things quietly and slowly ...*

Jessica's first response 'No' was based on her understanding of the verbal language; when probed further she mapped her understanding on to extralinguistic meanings as well.

When talking about her one-year-old twin sisters, Jessica shared her keen observations on how they are learning to talk:

Q: Do your sisters talk?

J: *Yes. Sometimes they say the same thing at the same time ... When they're hungry they open their mouths and go umumum ... When they're getting changed they cry because they want to go in the bath they like being in the bath ... When my mum takes the buggy out Sasi and Mattie both try to climb in ... When they play they talk a lot ... screaming as well, once Mattie said 'across'... They say many words, like mama, dada, at, Des (for Jess), ta, ... but I don't think they mean it ... I talk to them very quietly, because if you're loud they might cry ...*

Jessica understands how babies learn to talk. She has observed that her sisters practise sounds without necessarily relating them to meanings at this stage of their development. She understands that play produces a range of talk, using a variety of sounds, high and low. She also knows that babies signify meanings with actions associated with some random sounds and that verbal meanings are acquired later. Activities in the classroom, such as those suggested below, could help Jessica to become more explicit about the knowledge she has of language acquisition and to extend it further.

A child like Jessica might be considered monolingual on the surface – however, the opportunity to talk about language allows her to demonstrate her capacity to step outside and look at people's use of languages objectively. Opportunities such as this allow monolingual speakers to engage with language as a symbolic system (metalinguistic knowledge). She has gained this capacity through coming into contact with the different sounds of languages around her, including her own. Her interest in people has helped her to understand a great deal about the social uses of language (sociolinguistic knowledge).

Tom has just started secondary school in North London. His parents come from Birmingham and Scotland. Tom has a fascination for language; he likes talking about language.

> *'The thing about language is that it's so diverse in different ways that people use it … There are so many different languages out there that I think it'll probably be impossible to understand them all fully … I know personally a little bit of Italian* [Tom's uncle lives in Italy and his cousin speaks fluent Italian], *English and a tiny little Scottish English* [he understands more than he can say] *as I visit my family in Scotland often, and a tiny little French, which I'm learning at school. … Language is just a sort of mystery to me … Learning French in school I'm always learning something new and think how amazing the different words are, and the different phrases, how over time you can recognise different things … how they link up with words* [words and phrases in English].'

Here, Tom vividly substantiates his fascination for languages. He talks enthusiastically about the diversity of language in his own family and shows an openness to language learning, even though he has only minimal use of languages other than English. His experiences help him to understand the diverse ways of communicating meaning in different languages and to recognise the links between languages.

> Q: When did you first become aware of different languages?
> T: *First time I was aware that Scotland had its own language when my uncle said something like 'ok-ai' … Or my mum saying I'm going to get messages* [shopping] *from the shop, or a person who was always sad was such a 'dour'.*

His early contact with a new variety of English raises his awareness of linguistic diversity.

For Tom, as with Jessica, the links between language and social contact are very important. When asked about speakers of other languages in his class, he replied:

> *'Yes, my best friend is Raphaël, a French-speaking Swiss … he's fluent in French but not so in English … I think knowing another language makes you more sensitive to use language, it enhances your social abilities …'*

Tom is also very aware of the benefits of learning languages for his future. He perceives advantages in terms of personal gains and looking out at the world.

> Q: Why do you want to learn another language? In what ways do you think it would help you?
> T: *I'll benefit from it in the future. Say … France is about three times the size of England, say if nothing in England caught my eyes* [i.e. jobs], *I can happily go to France to look for one … Another language I'd like to learn is Mandarin, it's one of the hardest languages in the world … I'd like to travel to China – in fact quite a lot of the world …*

Nirmala (11) and her older sister **Namita** (14) are fluent Hindi-English bilinguals, both born and brought up in London. They enjoy close family ties with relations in India, which have enabled them to maintain and develop their knowledge of Hindi. When Namita was eleven, on one of her visits to India she was taught to read and write in Hindi by her cousins. She refers to them as 'cousin brothers and sisters', thus transferring the Hindi cultural meaning to English.

Speaking about her learning to write in Hindi, she says:

'They used to take me up to the terrace every evening (no one knew about it!) and teach me how to read and write … it wasn't very difficult to learn 'cos the spellings in Hindi are very regular, not like English … and I was able to read and write quickly …'

When Namita came back to London she surprised everyone by writing a letter to her grandfather in Hindi (below). The letter is full of family matters and expresses her emotional bond with Hindi.

Ms. Namita Gupta.

प्रिय बाबा,

आप सब कैसे हैं? सब कुछ ठीक ही चल रहा होगा। हम सर्वाँ ठीक हैं। मिथ्लेश दीदी की शादी कब हैं रखी है? हमारा इंडिया आने का प्रोग्राम अभी नहीं है। पापा की तबीयत ठीक चल रही है। दुगेश दीदी की अब तबीयत कैसी है? बाबा, आप अब कैसे हो? आप सब की बहुत याद आती है। निर्मला खूब रोती है। मनोज अब सैटल ही गया है। पापा इंडिया आने का विचार कर रहे हैं। आने की सूचना देंगे। कुकू की पढ़ाई कैसी चल रही है? मेरी हिंदी आप को कैसी लगी?

आप की बेटी
S. कुछ फोटो भेजे हैं। नमिता

Dear Baba,

How are you all? Everything must be fine. We are fine here. When is Mithlesh didi's [didi is a respectable addressee term] *wedding? We don't have any plans to come to India immediately. Papa's health is fine. How's Durgesh didi's health? We miss you all very much – Nirmala cries a lot. Manoj must be settled* [in his job] *by now. Papa is thinking of coming to India alone. He'll let you know when he comes. How's Kuku getting on with her studies? How do you like my Hindi?*

Aapki beti [Your daughter – cultural expression of family bond]

Namita

P.S. Have sent some photos.

Writing about people's mother tongue Fishman (1991: 4) noted: 'It is a very mystic, moving and powerful link with the past and an energiser with respect to the present and the future ... The destruction of a language is the destruction of a rooted identity ... intimacy, family and community.'

From a young age the sisters have used both English and Hindi. When Namita is asked whether she ever switches languages, she replies:

'Yes I do, when people know my languages ... When you speak in Hindi it sounds more homely ... Your language is unique to yourself ... Some words in Hindi haven't got English words, for example the 'respectful words' [addressee terms] *like,* didi [older sister]*,* bhayiya [older brother]*, and the names for different* [sets of] *aunts and uncles – in English they only say 'aunts' and 'uncles' ... . One day my friend Sade, an African Caribbean and her parents come from Trinidad, was talking to me on the phone when my younger sister kept on interrupting me and I asked her to 'shut up' and Sade said 'don't be mean to your sister'. I told her that she was 'disrespectful' to me, she doesn't even call me* 'didi' *and I explained her how things are in my language and culture. Sade agreed with me and said she should call me* 'didi'.*'*

In this extract, Namita articulates her knowledge of the cultural connotations of words in different languages and the emotional impact this can have on speakers. Namita obviously shows extensive insights into the inextricable relationship between language and culture. Namita's bilingualism has helped her to engage in metalinguistic thinking. She has retained the interest in language and languages which her early linguistic and cultural experiences have given her. It is interesting to note that her attainment in both English and French at secondary school has been very high.

Namita's sister Nirmala also shares the same interest in and knowledge of language and culture. When asked if she were paired with a friend who spoke another language, what she would want to learn from her and teach her, she gives an enthusiastic reply:

'Oh that's interesting! I'd like to learn Turkish, 'cos I've got a Turkish friend ... I'd want her to teach me 'basics', like how to greet each other; Are there different ways of greeting friends and 'respectable' people, like older people? Like in Hindi you say 'hello' or 'hi' to cousins and friends but 'namaste' to respectful people ... [I would like her to teach me] *some Turkish expressions, how to talk and dress politely if I go to Turkey. Perhaps learn some songs and everyday conversations, like, 'How are you?' 'Where do you live?' 'How old are you?' ' What do you enjoy doing the most?' How to use the street map and transport ...'*
Q: And what will you teach her?
N: I'll teach her everything I just said and I'll teach her some Bollywood [movies in Hindi from Bombay] *songs and dances ... she can learn a lot of Hindi from that ... I'll teach her about Indian traditional clothes and our Hindu gods and festivals and how to talk politely ... so that she doesn't offend anybody ...*

Like her sister, Nirmala engages at an emotional level when talking about language. Many language learning studies show that 'emotions are seen as vital' (Johnstone 1993).

Q: Namita, what do you think is the best way of learning a new language?

N: *You should talk to them a lot ... In school they teach you individual words ... Not as a connected sentence ... Talking gives you practice and builds up your confidence ... we should have pronunciation practice and discussion and basically try to speak the language ...*

In the above discussions the young people are showing knowledge of language acquisition, language varieties, awareness of other languages, thoughts about how to learn languages, verbal and non-verbal communication, social uses of language, as well as links between language and identity and language and culture. Giving children the opportunity to articulate their knowledge in this way can help their conceptualisation of what language is and motivates them to learn other languages. Because they are talking about very personal experiences, they are also showing how language and identity are inextricably linked. The opportunity to articulate and reflect on their experiences in class discussions reinforces their own identity and gives value to the languages and varieties that are closest to them.

 ## GETTING PUPILS TO TALK ABOUT LANGUAGE

The suggestions below show a number of ways of instigating class discussions about language and cultural diversity.

MAKING AUDIO OR VIDEO TAPES

Teachers, pupils and parents can make audio or video tapes of interviews about language, similar to those shown in the extracts above. Ideally the tapes would include examples of words, phrases, songs, etc, in different languages and language varieties. The tapes can then be used as a basis of classroom discussion.

The following is a list of example questions, which could be used as a starting point for talking about language with children. It is best if children decide for themselves what they want to know and then form their own questions for the taped interviews. Further questions will arise from the responses. It is important to structure an interview, but also to allow interviewers to follow lines of enquiry as they arise. Work of this kind needs a supportive classroom ethos where children can talk freely about issues which are very personal and sensitive. There is further discussion of how to plan and achieve this in Chapter 2.

BRING AND TELL

During Circle Time in the primary classroom pupils can focus on different languages by bringing in personal artefacts or photographs (including holiday photographs), which relate to different languages and cultures. This provides opportunities for talking about the speakers and sounds of these languages and for exploring and sharing what the children in the class understand about them. The teacher can ask questions such as 'Do you know any of these languages? Can you say anything in this language?' Teachers can take this further and encourage language sharing and language comparisons. The teacher could start this by modelling it her or himself – for example, bringing a photograph of a relative or friend who uses another language and talking about the person and the language, exchanging some common expressions in the language, or bringing a holiday photograph to talk about her or his language and cultural experiences.

INVITING PARENTS

Teachers could invite parents into the classroom for discussion about language. For example, a parent could bring in a storybook, poster or newspaper in another language and read it and share the content with the children. Single words or phrases common in several languages and used in the text could be pointed out and learned by the class. Children could collect examples of writing in different languages and scripts for a 'calligraphy corner' (see Chapter 5).

PAIRED LANGUAGE TEACHING

In a multilingual classroom teachers could organise paired language teaching. For example, teaching simple greetings and exchanges of personal information – name, age, how are you, where you live, etc. Nirmala suggests many possibilities above. Also, many books are available to support these activities (see examples on left).Young learners want language learning to be fun and linguistic concepts can be shared between friends in a supportive emotional environment. Children can also be encouraged by teachers or parents to learn and share some simple rhymes, songs and proverbs. Here is a traditional rhyme in Turkish:

Küçük kurbağa	*Little frog*
Küçük kurbağa	*Little frog*
Ellerin nerede?	*Where are your hands?*
Ellerim yok	*I don't have hands*
Ellerim yok	*I don't have hands*
Yüzerim derede	*I swim in the pond.*
Küçük kurbağa	*Little frog*
Küçük kurbağa	*Little frog*
Kuyruğun nerede?	*Where is your tail?*
Kuyruğum yok	*I don't have a tail*
Kuyruğum yok	*I don't have a tail*
Yüzerim derede	*I swim in the pond.*

LANGUAGE SURVEYS

Children can be encouraged to collect information about languages using various types of survey. Some examples of surveys are shown below.

A good way to start is by getting children to collect or brainstorm names of different languages or language varieties they have heard of. Completing an 'A to Z' of languages is a useful way to structure this, especially in a less multilingual classroom. This brings languages alive because it allows children to validate their personal knowledge and experience. Children can research to find names of languages and language varieties beginning with each letter of the alphabet. It is useful if the teacher has a reference book (such as Katzner's *The Languages of the world* 2002) to check the languages and to find out where they are used.

A to Z of Languages

A

B

Cantonese: Sui Mi's family is from Hong Kong, she speaks Cantonese fluently and is learning to write it.

D

E

F

Gujerati: Herna understands Gujerati as her grandparents speak it at home. She's learning to speak and read Gujerati.

H

I

J

K

L

M

N

O

P

Q

R

Somali: Faduma was born in Somalia, and speaks and writes Somali and English.

T

U

V

W

X

Y

Z

When children have identified as many languages and language varieties as possible on the chart, they could begin noting names of speakers (friends, classmates, famous people, family members) or making notes of when and where they have come in contact with these languages or sticking on the chart written examples of the languages. A world map on the wall can help children locate the origins of these languages and think about how languages travel.

The European Language Portfolio (CILT 2001) provides an appealing format for getting pupils to record their own language uses. It is also useful to get children to record the languages used by other members of the family or friends, languages they would like to learn or languages found in the local neighbourhood (in the library, shops, community centres, etc). While linguistic diversity is being celebrated in this way, children can also reflect on the languages they would like to learn in the future and the reasons. Children can design their own creative ways of collecting and recording information.

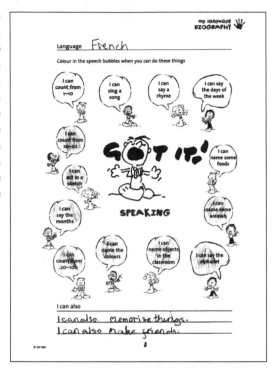

My Family's Languages

Person	Language
Paulo (my cousin)	Portuguese
Ana (my cousin)	Portuguese

Languages I would like to learn

Language	Reason
Portuguese	Because I liked going on holiday in Portugal (Jessica)

Languages in the neighbourhood

Place/person	Language	Example
My next door neighbour Samira	Urdu and Arabic	Perhaps a cutting from a newspaper or photocopy of print from a book

CLASS LANGUAGE BOOKS

A class language book can contain pupils' research, thoughts and writings about language, examples of different languages, poems, songs, rhymes, proverbs, etc as a celebratory record. For example, Fanoula Xeneki, a student teacher working with a class of seven and eight year-olds in a school in Hackney in London, made 'Our languages book'. Below is a collaborative poem from the book:

Greetings

These are the ways we say hello,
And put smiles on the faces of those we know
Ola *in Spanish,* bonjour *in French*
In Bengali it's keeta aachen *or* swagatum,
In Arabic, salam-alay-kum
How many other ways can we greet,
And put smiles on the faces of those we meet?
How are you? In Tigran it's Te-me-le-ki?
If you say Ti kanete? *You'll be speaking Greek.*
But rather than find out from a book
We can tell you in 3B
If you're fine in Greek you say kala,
In Tigran, tobuk.
When we meet we say hi!
When we leave we say goodbye,
Adios, au revoir, zagee,
Is what you will hear from class 3B!

(Datta, 2000: 36)

This chapter has shown ways of getting children to talk about their personal experiences and perceptions of language and languages as a way of celebrating diversity of language and culture. The initial interest and curiosity generated by the activities suggested in this chapter can then be followed up by looking at the different aspects of language covered in Chapters 3–6. The next chapter will discuss some of the issues teachers need to consider in their management and organisation of multilingual approaches to language teaching.

2. Managing multilingual activities

This chapter aims to help teachers to manage multilingual classroom activities in order to create positive attitudes towards language learning by showing:

- the importance of affective (emotional) factors in the language learning process;

- the powerful links between language, culture and identity;

- the importance of cross-cultural communications and the issues involved;

- ways of developing positive teacher attitudes and teaching approaches;

- ways of collaborating with adult speakers of other languages to plan and teach together.

AFFECTIVE FACTORS IN LANGUAGE LEARNING

Robert, a Year 7 pupil in a London school, was lining up outside the classroom awaiting his first French lesson at his new secondary school. He had 'a face of thunder' and when the teacher asked him what was upsetting him he burst out with an angry rant saying ' I can't do French, I don't know any French, why do I have to learn French?' The teacher had to muster all her skills to ensure that Robert overcame whatever insecurities and misunderstandings had fired this negative attitude so that he could begin to enjoy language learning and achieve in this new subject. Although this is an extreme example, it is not untypical of the low self-esteem and attitudinal blocks to language learning that pupils and teachers can face. Such highly emotional attitudes can be formed at an early age if pupils are not given sensitive guidance and positive opportunities and experiences that stimulate their curiosity and openness to other languages and cultures and build their confidence to learn.

Stephen Krashen, an American writer and researcher in the field of second language acquisition, emphasises the importance of affective factors in language learning. He uses the metaphor of an 'affective filter' which can impede language acquisition and learning if learners feel anxious, lacking in confidence or uncomfortable in the learning situation. According to Krashen (1982), when the 'affective filter' (anxiety level) is down, learners can absorb the language input in the environment, which will allow internal language processes to work. However when the filter is up, learners' anxiety or lack of confidence blocks this process. Many other researchers in this field (for example, Spolsky (1989), Schumann (1978), Cummins (1996) and Datta (2000)) emphasise the effect of attitudes towards the target language and culture on achievement in language learning.

Primary teachers, therefore, have a crucial role to play in ensuring that pupils develop the confidence and positive attitudes to languages that will motivate them to learn languages in the future. Without positive action to counter society's often negative or indifferent attitudes to other languages, cultures or bilingual speakers, teachers can unwittingly accept or reinforce these and thereby block children's potential for language learning.

LANGUAGE, CULTURE AND IDENTITY

Most adults can recount occasions in their lives when they have become acutely aware of their own use of language and its close links with their sense of individual identity. These occasions occur when their language use may have made them feel particularly embarrassed or proud or they may have consciously modified or changed their language use in order to 'fit in'. These occasions may be triggered by situations when their use of language has been approved, praised, laughed at or criticised or by moving to a new environment where a different language or language variety (accent or dialect) is used. The emotional impact of such occasions can be very deep – a perceived criticism of one's language use, for example, can feel like a very personal insult, which can then affect self-esteem for a very long time. Teachers can counter this kind of effect by doing language and identity awareness-raising activities which ensure that children feel good about themselves and their languages and look positively towards future language learning.

In order to achieve this, teachers' own awareness of the powerful links between language and identity is very important. A useful staff development exercise to raise awareness is to ask teachers to reflect on their own language history in pairs, using such questions as:

What languages and varieties of English have you used in your life? What do you feel about each of these? Which is closest to your personal identity?

Where are these languages and varieties normally spoken? Who normally uses them? Are they used differently in different contexts or with different groups of people?

Are there any times in your life when you have become very aware of your language use? Why was this? How did this affect you?

This exercise usually works best if the person leading the activity starts off by talking about his or her own experience, highlighting how they identify with the different languages and language varieties used and explaining why.

As part of this reflective exercise, teachers could produce a visual representation of their language histories (for example, a timeline) to present to others. These exercises can then lead to further discussion of the ways in which language and identity and language and social status are linked. This can deepen teachers' awareness of linguistic diversity among even seemingly homogenous communities as well as of some of the principles and social patterns related to language variety and change.

Represented overleaf is the timeline of Tanya's language history. It shows very clearly how learning languages is an asset at many levels.

Tanya's language history

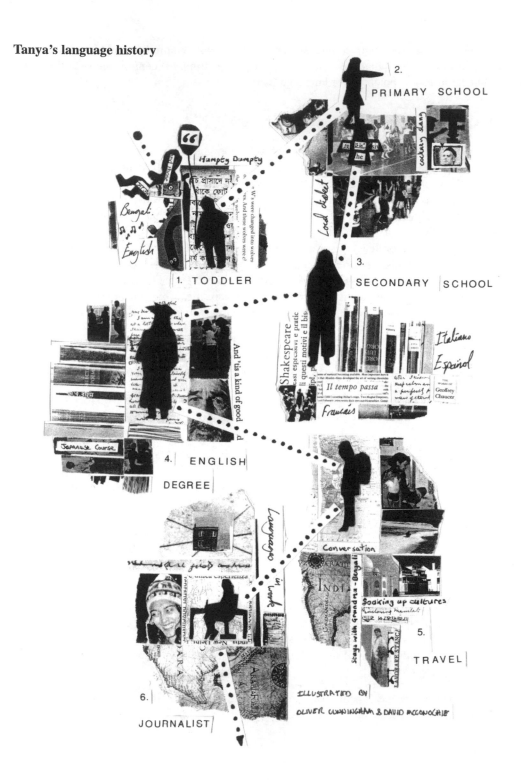

These exercises help teachers not only to enjoy sharing their language histories but also to experience first hand the sensitivity needed for language-sharing activities. The example below was written by a pupil from a school in Hackney in London and shows the emotional impact of moving to a new linguistic environment:

> **It felt like being a baby all over again**
>
> *I learnt lots of basic words at the age of nine to ten months. My mother thought that I learnt these words at quite an early age because of my sister, who was four at the time. My mother said that she used to talk to me and tell me stories like I could understand everything that she was saying. Also at that time my mother was thinking of taking my sister off to start the nursery, so what she used to do was to teach my sister how to read. My mum said that because she was teaching her how to read she used to come into my playroom and practise how to read it well so that she would get it right when reading it to my mum and dad.*
>
> *All of this talking and communicating with me when I was small probably was the reason why I developed a language skill at quite an early age.*
>
> *When I was eight years old my mother and father decided that they wanted to move to Portugal to live. When they told me and my sister Carla about their plans I was devastated. I knew that I had to go with them though. When we got to Portugal I used to get very short-tempered, because it used to annoy me when people talked to my mum and dad and I could not understand them. As time went on I started to learn basic things to get by. Really, it felt like being a baby all over again, not knowing what people are saying to you, not being able to reply in case you said something wrong, making a fool of yourself.*
>
> Suraya Klein-Smith – published in *The voice inside* (Hackney Education and Leisure 1994)

Because of this emotional (and sometimes even traumatic) experience pupils can be reluctant or reserved in sharing their language knowledge with others. It can take a long time to build the trust necessary to enable pupils to disclose to others the details of their language histories. Thus the importance of creating and managing a secure and collaborative classroom environment for language work cannot be overstated.

CROSS-CULTURAL COMMUNICATIONS

The potential difficulties of cross-cultural communications have frequently been commented upon. Studies such as those of Gumperz (1982) show how difficult it can be for those perceived to have a lower social status, including speakers of minority languages, to feel that they have a 'voice' in an educational setting dominated by a powerful global language such as Standard English. It is important that teachers are aware of these social attitudes and work to challenge them, adding new meaning to language learning through activities such as those suggested in this book.

Those who have had some experience of having to adapt to living in a new language and culture are often much more aware of the potential for misunderstandings and miscommunications, including different perceptions of what is rude and what is socially acceptable in terms of language and social behaviour. Ben-Zeev (1977) shows how children who use more than one language in their lives naturally develop a 'communicative sensitivity' towards other language speakers and language use. For example, Namita in Chapter 1 wanted to know how to talk respectfully in Turkish to adults. This sensitivity is an invaluable asset for learning languages and for understanding the complexity of what language is. Teachers therefore need to find ways of developing this communicative sensitivity among all children, including those with limited access to other languages and language varieties.

If you have a choice of language or language variety, this means that you can select the most suitable way of expressing your meaning for a particular context or audience. In most parts of the world it is very normal to hear and expect to use more than one language on an everyday basis. Below is an example of first experiences of England of an adult from India:

> ... it was not until I came to England that I became 'aware' of being a multilingual. I must say I found it hard to relate to the term, because not only did I think multilingualism was the norm but until then I had not thought of my languages as different or separate entities. Growing up and educated multilingually, all my languages – Bengali, Punjabi, Hindi, English – served different social functions. (Datta 2000: 1)

The predominance of English throughout the world makes it possible for children in this country to grow up with very limited contact with other languages. Even when surrounded by users of other languages, children can easily hear only English being used around them. This is because speakers of other languages often feel pressured to accommodate to English even when they share another language. The resulting lack of exposure to linguistic variety and the lack of intellectually stimulating talk about language which goes with it, can have the unfortunate effect of blocking children's language learning potential and depriving them of opportunities to develop an important social dimension.

While it is essential that children in this country learn to be proficient in Standard English, it is also important that this variety of English is perceived as a language among many other languages and language varieties in the world, all of which have subtle and sophisticated ways of communicating meanings. An openness and curiosity about different languages and language varieties can be established in the primary years through enjoyable language learning experiences which are personally meaningful to children; it is more likely that children will then expect and welcome the opportunity to learn other languages in future. This is the principle underlying all the activities outlined in this book. The remainder of this chapter looks at how teachers who may be monolingual themselves can nevertheless use approaches and strategies which help to develop a sensitivity and openness to other languages and cultures.

TEACHING APPROACHES

INCLUSION

The voices of the children in Chapter 1 were stimulated by a teacher who in her words and intonation, as well as her facial expression and body language, showed enthusiasm for the language and cultural experiences of these children. For example, when Namita and Nirmala talked about their cousins in India, the teacher's encouraging nods and smiles showed her genuine interest in their experiences and helped them to reflect more deeply as they shared their stories with her. The teacher's attitude when discussing language varieties and personal experiences is crucial as it often has to challenge the assumptions and negative attitudes of society at large which may have already affected children. This is why many children in school deny that they know another language. Without the conviction and positive attitude of the teacher interviewing them, children such as Tom (p5) or Jessica (p4) could easily feel that they do not have very much to say about other languages. However, the teacher's interest and enthusiastic and supportive questions helped to engage them in the topic, making them want to reflect and share what they know. Equally children like Suraya (p17) could worry that talking about different languages might bring back uncomfortable memories and be reluctant to share their knowledge and experience with others. Children such as Namita and Nirmala (p6) might assume that their teacher does not think that reading and writing in Hindi is as important or valuable as literacy in English. One way of gaining children's trust to talk about their language experiences is for the teacher to act as a model by telling children about his or her own personal language history, including some of the feelings which he or she experienced as a result of different language uses and language change. A teacher giving a Year 6 class their first few lessons in French before they transferred to her secondary school said:

'I started by asking how many of them could teach me another language. About six children shyly raised their hands, obviously a bit unsure how their peers would react. I told them some stories about my own learning of French and then taught them to say a few words about themselves in French. We all enjoyed an active language lesson. After a few lessons, I was surrounded by a crowd of enthusiastic children who wanted to tell me more about the languages and dialects they knew. I don't think anyone had asked them that question before and afterwards I tried to find ways of constantly referring to the knowledge they brought with them to the language class. I learned so much from them and I think it helped them to know that I was interested in their language as well as teaching them mine.'

MANAGING INTERACTIVE LANGUAGE ACTIVITIES

PRINCIPLES

The other chapters in this book contain a number of examples of activities involving interaction between children, such as the games and role play activities in Chapter 5 'Doing language'. Given the importance of the affective factors discussed above, teachers need to manage these interactions with care. Firstly, setting clear boundaries is important to ensure that an appropriate ethos of respect for all languages and cultures is created and maintained. This will encourage all children to be motivated to share their knowledge and experience. The following principles can inform the setting of boundaries for managing multilingual language activities in the classroom:

- Language knowledge is shared equally among teachers and learners; everyone should feel good about contributing their own knowledge and experience to this process.

- Language development and social interactions are interdependent, as the activities in this book demonstrate. Therefore learning tasks should be planned to include social exchanges in which children share their personal experiences, their cultural and linguistic identities and their historical heritage.

- Linguistically all languages and language varieties enjoy equal status. This notion challenges the perceived differences of status resulting from different power positions in society.

GROUPING

Given these principles, teachers need to consider the best ways to group or pair children. Friendship groups or pairs are important to ensure learning takes place in an enjoyable and stress-free environment. Sometimes, however teachers may want to change groups or pairs based on their knowledge of the potential of individual learners. Some of the strategies suggested by the National Oracy Project (1990) are very useful for regrouping children for different purposes.

The strategy below is described in the National Oracy Project advice for Key Stage One teachers (p14). It could be used for a number of language tasks where different pieces of information need to be collected or different language tasks (songs, role plays, etc) need to be practised:

A structure for groups which ensures that every child has a role is known as 'Jigsaw'. The basic principle is that children have a 'home' group where they start and finish and an 'expert' group, which they join to do their investigation.

For example: the class is going to find out about materials that dissolve in water. The children go into self-chosen 'home' groups of five, discuss what sorts of things they might be going to do and number off. Then all the children with the same number become an 'expert' group with one particular investigation to do. When the 'expert' group has finished, the members agree on their findings and then go back to the 'home' group where each child, of course, is an 'expert' on his or her experiment and has to play a full part in the bringing together of the information.

Jigsawing can be used for any work which requires children to study something together, and which can be 'broken' into parts to be brought together again. It can also be applied to short- or long-term activities.

TASKS

Language learning tasks in any classroom should be interactive, as suggested throughout the book, based on children's shared interests and experiences. Tasks should be constructed in such a way that children take responsibility to learn and move on to broaden their personal boundaries. For example, sharing their knowledge and experiences of festivals, children may want to further their shared knowledge by researching in books, talking to significant adults and others, taking part in concerts or other events – the work in the classroom is just the beginning of this learning process. In this way the interest and inspiration is taken further beyond the classroom into communities, libraries, outings, travels, etc.

 ## COLLABORATING WITH BILINGUAL ADULTS IN PLANNING AND TEACHING

A class teacher cannot be expected to have knowledge of all the languages and language varieties which could be used in the classroom. It is important, therefore, that teachers find strategies for informing themselves about languages as well as ways of team teaching and planning with bilingual adults who could help them bring linguistic diversity into their classrooms. Where teaching assistants are bilingual they can be an invaluable linguistic resource for language work with children.

Once a teacher becomes 'attuned' to the idea of exploring linguistic and cultural diversity, a number of hitherto unexpected opportunities and materials can arise. Hearing other languages and language varieties being used by parents or teaching staff in the school as well as catering staff, school caretakers, teaching assistants, etc, could present an opportunity for a teacher to enquire further and think about possible ways of introducing the language or language variety to the class. Teachers can also gain information about the languages used in the local community, for example in shops or community centres. A local shopkeeper used to greet children regularly in Gujerati after he found out that a particular teacher had been learning some Gujerati with her class. The class started learning Gujerati from a parent and a group of Gujerati-speaking children in order to be able to greet a new pupil who was arriving from India to join the class. Imagine the child's surprise when her new classmates in an English school greeted her and asked her questions in her own language about her name, her age and where she lived. She was delighted!

Bilingual adults are a very rich resource, but working with them in the classroom to ensure that everyone benefits positively needs sensitivity, thought and preparation. On the one hand it is important to give children some first hand contact with native speakers of the language in question in order to gain a rich cultural and linguistic experience. On the other hand thought needs to be given to how children might respond to a visitor to their classroom who is using an unfamiliar language.

It is important to remember that such adults may not be teachers themselves or may have experience of teaching in very different contexts and thus may find direct communication with the class to be very challenging. Experienced teachers often operate so intuitively that they forget how skilled and knowledgeable you need to be to manage classroom activity. It takes a fair amount of teaching and communication skill and a good deal of knowledge of the individuals to be able to mediate between a visitor to the class and the children in it. This is particularly challenging when the visitor is using a language or language variety that may be unfamiliar to many of the children and to the teacher.

One of the best ways to address this is to consider beforehand how the children will get to know the bilingual visitor. This could involve talking openly with the children about people's 'sensitivity' to their own language and culture. Ideally, before embarking on a language learning task, the bilingual visitor should be present in the classroom, getting to know the children by observing, helping and participating in activities, particularly activities with role play and talk. This could be followed by a 'getting to know the visitor' session. In this session the children could ask the visitor about his or her family, childhood, interests, as well as his or her life in Britain and relationships abroad (if any), leading on to questions about the language and culture. Teachers should meet with the bilingual visitor to plan together beforehand the language and activities to be introduced (a song, poem, dance, greetings, etc) before embarking on a class activity. In this way the teacher can learn some language from the visitor before using it in class. The teacher can then participate in using the language and help with the communication and management of the activity.

It is hard to achieve a balance between ensuring effective classroom communication and management and a sufficiently rich exposure to the target language and culture. It requires commitment, tact and understanding to get it right, but the social, linguistic and cultural benefits to children can be enormous.

The teacher described above, who learned Gujerati with her class, prepared for this by working with a parent and a group of Gujerati-speaking pupils in the school. Together they prepared videotape and accompanying tasks to teach the class greetings, numbers and simple social exchanges in Gujerati. While the parent and pupils prepared the language materials, the teacher researched for photographs and maps from which the class learned where Gujerati is spoken, both locally, in different parts of Britain, and in India and other countries.

When talking to the parent, the teacher discovered her interest in stories and dance; together they planned a story-telling session for the class. The story was told in Gujerati but with some English phrases interspersed that allowed the children to participate equally. Following this, to the teacher's delight, the parent agreed to teach 'Garba', a springtime group dance with sticks and with some very structured footsteps and lively music which children found immensely enjoyable and easy to follow. The children shared and enjoyed a rich language learning experience from this contact.

This chapter has shown the importance of informed and sensitive management of multilingual classroom activities and has given examples of ways of working with bilingual adults in bringing different languages and cultures into the classroom, enabling children to share and learn from each other. The following chapters show how this can be done through language learning activities.

3. Multilingual stories and text level work

This chapter aims to:

- show that stories offer excellent resources for language learning and enjoyment;

- show how reading and role playing stories from diverse language and cultural backgrounds add to children's cognitive development as well as language learning possibilities;

- expand children's confidence and thinking as users or learners of language through some story-based activities for teachers in any classroom by:
  - showing the links and interaction between setting, characters and events;
  - showing the interrelationship between language and culture;
  - enabling children to understand the universal nature of story structures across languages and cultures through interesting activities.

UNIVERSAL APPEAL OF STORIES

Stories in any language provide very powerful models for language learning. Teachers in the primary and early years classroom understand the importance of stories, rhymes and songs for children's language development. The National Literacy Strategy puts great emphasis on analysing story settings, characters, events, language and structure from Year 1. Children relate to stories emotionally and imaginatively as well as aurally – these sensual experiences stimulate their language learning potential. In this chapter we will look at how stories can be used as an enjoyable and meaningful resource to build children's knowledge about story as a form of language. This knowledge is strengthened if children are exposed to stories from a range of cultures.

HOW DO STORIES HELP LANGUAGE LEARNING?

Children usually come to school carrying a range of stories and their rhythms and sound patterns in their heads. These stories are inextricably linked with cultural experiences and cultural items (artefacts) that are familiar to them. Many children will be familiar with folk or fairy tales. The story of Cinderella's lost 'shoe' had its origin in China where small feet are a sign of nobility and beauty in a woman. The story associated with 'small feet' as a cultural artefact and its symbolic representation travelled from China to almost every part of the world. Most readers have come across Aesop's fables, which are the most travelled stories in the world and have successfully adapted to the cultural artefacts of the countries they travelled. For example, the story of the crow and the pitcher: when told in India, the crow becomes a *kowaa* and the shape of the pitcher changes to the shape of an Indian *matka,* a pot with a narrow neck and a very round bottom. Hilary Hester (1983) notes the magical power of stories to provide continuity between generations and make links between people and societies when she says 'Stories are like spells not only for adults and children, but also across time and cultures'. Some children have such stories in their heads in other languages or language varieties. This knowledge and cultural memory needs to be validated for all children in school if it is to help them build further language learning.

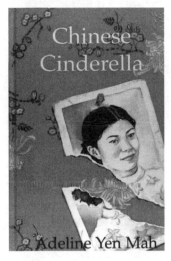

All children respond to rhythmic groupings of words and sounds, no matter what language they are hearing. For example, young bilingual learners of English in many schools enjoy stories such as *We're going on a bear hunt* (Rosen and Oxenbury 1989, see Chapter 5 as well) or *Mr Gumpy's outing* (Burningham 1970), because the rhyme, rhythm and repetitions in these texts help them to access the meaning of the story as well as memorise the language patterns and grammatical structures in a fun way. The memorised patterns help create further linguistic patterns with new vocabulary items. Similarly stories with rhythm, repetition and a refrain in other languages can be understood and enjoyed by children not familiar with the language. Edwards (1998:44) describes a Punjabi story-teller who tells stories in his first language to mostly native-English speaking pupils. At the end of the session the story-teller said 'They couldn't understand what I was saying [*the words*], but they could grasp what was going on – they could pick up the vibes [*the whole experience of the story*].' The children who participated in this story-telling session learned that story grammar is universal, that stories in other languages communicate meanings and feelings which are just as enjoyable as stories in English. They picked up some of the sounds and intonation of the language and the emotional satisfaction gave them a positive self concept and motivation to learn more of the language. The session helped them to feel comfortable with hearing and learning a new language and showed them how non-verbal communicative strategies such as mime, gesture, facial expression, tone, intonation, etc can support verbal meanings in an unfamiliar language. This experience provides excellent preparation for learning other languages in the future.

Therefore, we must find ways of using this rich and very fluid cultural and linguistic resource for further learning and new language learning possibilities. Stories were an important aspect of language development in the case study of a six year-old Bengali girl called Nadia living in the borough of Tower Hamlets. (See Datta 2000: 58–76). From speaking mostly Bengali with very little English at the start of the study, Nadia became a fluent speaker and reader of English over the seven-month duration of the study. At the heart of this development was her love for narratives in Bengali and English. Throughout the case study Nadia carried a pile of books with her that her teacher and friend Samia had read. These books in English and Bengali were a precious treasure for Nadia that spanned both her 'worlds' and motivated her to read fluently in a remarkably short period of time.

In another case a student teacher told a story about a donkey and a carrot in Bengali to a class of six-year-old mostly monolingual (native-English speaking) children. She had carefully chosen a text with rhythmic grouping of words and repetitive patterns which, together with use of magnetic pictures as well as voice, tone and facial expression, helped convey the meaning and bring the story alive. The children were spellbound by the narrative and inundated her with comments and questions about the story and about the language. One boy, a native speaker of English, said he particularly enjoyed the sound and rhythm of the words '*choltey-choltey, choltey-choltey*' (meaning 'walking-walking, walking-walking') told in a high and low voice to show the rhythm of the donkey's continuous walking following the carrot in front of his head. The child moved his finger in the air to show the rhythmic pattern and the high and low tone of voice – this shows a deep understanding of the phonology of this language. Everyone agreed with him that this was the best part of the story and started imitating the sounds and rhythm of '*choltey-choltey*'.

A Sri Lankan child in the same group said to the student teacher 'In Bengali you say '*pani*' and in Tamil (the child's home language) we say '*tanni*' it's funny, they sound the same!' Both '*pani*' and '*tanni*', mean 'water'. The children's comments show they are becoming aware of metalinguistic concepts such as:

- how languages have different sets of sounds, some of which may not exist in their first language;
- that objects can have different names in different languages, that there may be similarities and differences in words, sounds and meanings between languages;
- how meaning is made in all languages through combinations of sounds, words, sentences and texts;
- how stylistic features, for example alliteration, onomatopoeia, repetition, pace and rhythm add to enjoyment and meaning in a story in any language.

Readers may note that all of these are featured strongly in the learning objectives of the National Literacy Strategy.

The resources and activities below show some examples of how teachers can bring multilingual stories into the classroom.

Examples of activities

Bilingual story-telling or reading

The teacher tells, reads and enacts a story in English using story props, tone, intonation, gestures and expression to support the meaning of the story. A parent or other adults, for example, a student teacher, support teacher, teaching assistant can retell the story in another language, preferably a community language represented in the class or neighbourhood using the same non-verbal strategies. This will need some practice and preparation (see Chapter 2, 'Managing multilingual activities'). The story could then be discussed by the class, guided by teacher questions such as those suggested below:

- Did you enjoy the story? What helped you to understand the story? It is important to emphasise enjoyment **first** as the emotional engagement helps children to think deeply about their understandings. 'One's emotions, imagination and intellect mutually support and enrich one another. Our positive feelings strengthen our rationality.' (Bettelheim 1976: 4).

- How did it sound in [name of language] and how does this compare with English? Can you identify some common features in both languages (for example, sounds, rhythm, etc)?

- Do you remember any words or sound patterns used in the story? What effect did the sound pattern create?

- Children should also be encouraged to ask their own questions and offer their own interpretations of how they understood the story.

- Children could learn and practise some phrases and expressions with the bilingual speaker.

Code-switching in stories

Alternatively, a story could be read or told in English but with some words or phrases in another language. For example, the story *A balloon for Grandad* by Nigel Gray can be adapted so that the balloon travels to different grandads or great-grandads, in different parts of the world (including Britain) and is greeted in different languages and regional varieties by them.

The extracts below show a teacher's translation of sentences from the English text into Russian.

A balloon for Grandad

It was bobbing and bumping in the breeze.
Он качался и стакал на ветерке.
On kachalsa ee stakal na veterke.

After breakfast.
После завтрака.
Posle zavtraka.

"Look! There goes your balloon," he said.
«Смотри! Там твой шарик,» он сказал.
« Smotri! Tam tvoy sharik,» on skazal.

It flew zig-zag up a cliff.
Полетел зигзагом на скалу.
Poletyel zigzagom na skaloo.

"No!" said the wind. "It's mine."
«Нет!» сказал ветер. «Это мой.»
«Nyet!» skazal veter. «Eto moy.»

"My balloon is going to visit Granddad Abdullah."
«Мой шарик посетит Дедушку Абдуллу.»
«Moy sharik posyeteet Dedooshkoo Abdulloo.»

CULTURE AND STORIES

Teachers can tell or read a story from another culture in English using visual props, tone intonation and expression to support the meaning. A good example of a story based in another culture is *Muhamed's desert night* by Cristina Kessler, which is the story of a Tuareg boy from North Africa. Although the story is written in English, the names of the characters, the day to day activities (e.g. meals, etc) and the setting are all very culturally specific and different from Western cultures. The way of expressing what is important in desert life, such as 'Leave no path, disturb no rock … make no changes on the earth, the desert is fair to someone who knows how to live with it' shows how people in this culture think about and express their own values and their connection to their environment. The advice given to Muhamed, the Tuareg boy, by his grandmother: 'You are the best of all. The strongest, the most handsome, a true camel man' conveys the pride and sense of identity communicated through the generations of Tuaregs.

> I taste the wind on my tongue
> and feels the sun touch my heart
> as finally I sit with my goats while they graze
> Yes, I am the wealthiest of boys.
>
> The desert is my floor. The rocks, my pasture
> where water gathers and little plants grow.
> There my goats can graze.
> 'Be at one with your surroundings and you will be at
> peace', my grandmother always says.
> Al Hamdillilai!

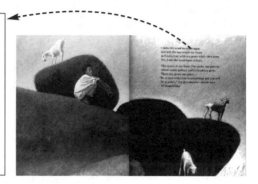

Possible questions to bring out the cultural values and identity in a story such as this could include:

- Is there anything in the story setting or characters that tells you that the story is from another part of the world? What are they? List them in clusters, e.g. setting, characters, action/events, names, etc. This relates well to the objectives in the National Literacy Strategy for text level work. For example, Year 5 Term 3: '1. Investigate a range of texts from different cultures, considering patterns of relationships, social customs, attitudes and beliefs'.
- Can you remember or find anything about the language used (different ways of saying things) which might show that the story is from another culture? Do you find these expressions interesting? What does this tell you about people and languages?
- What does the story tell you about the way of life of some people in that country? How does it compare with people's ways of life in Britain? (If a traditional story is used children need to be reminded that the costume or other cultural markers, for example, dwellings, etc, belong to that era rather than to contemporary times).
- Do you think the story will be interesting without these cultural features or artefacts?

USE OF HUMOUR IN STORIES ACROSS CULTURES

Humorous stories such as *Anancy* (Caribbean), *Hoca* (Turkish) or *Brer Rabbit* (American) provide enormous fun and talking points for comparison of what makes a character funny in different cultures.

STORIES AND FESTIVALS

Heritage stories related to different cultural festivals can be used to make class storybooks with children's illustrations or photographs of celebrations with family and friends. Another way of doing this is to share children's experiences and ideas around celebration of festivals in different cultures and making class books with pictures or photographs. Common expressions or names of people and objects in different languages can be used in these. Parents' involvement in this can be valuable.

Ana Mohamed, Ebn Arahid, Ebn Zainab
Akhon Le etnain banat wa talata dokoor,
koluhum Assihaa.
Ana Aghna Adokoor.
Nahno Atawarig, Albardo yakooloona
Anasso Azzorko.
Ayamona talodao maa toloi Ashamsse.
wa tantahi maa Egetimaina fi halakatee
hawla Anare Alati tasstao fi Sawad Assahraa.
AL hamdo LiLLah.

أنا محمد ، ابن أراحيد ، ابن زينب
أخ لـ شئن بنات و ثلا ثة ذكور، كلهم أصحاء،
أنا أغنى الذكور.
نحنا التوارك ، البعض يقولون الناس الزرق.
أيامنا تبدأ مع طلوع الشمس
و تنتهي مع اجتماعنا في حلقة حول النار
التي نسمع في سواد الصحراى
الحمد لله.

Son ابن Ebn
Brother أخ Akhoon
Day يوم Yawm
Campfires حلقة حول النار Halakatoon hawla Anar
Desert الصحراء Assahrao
Night ليل Lailoo.
Tuaregs are the princes of the Earth
التوارك هم أمراء الأرض
Atawareg hom Omarao ALardi.

MAKING STORY PROPS AND BOOKS

Following the reading of a story, for example, *Muhamed's desert night*, children can make props, e.g. drums, maps, models of animals, rocks, etc, or find other ways of retelling the story (e.g. role play/drama) in English, but inserting the words and phrases learned in the new language. Asking questions about children's feelings, enjoyment and learning in response to a story are very important aspects of language learning.

Children can make their own bilingual storybook in pairs, with a few words such as their names (as authors), important story features, for example, the title of the story, *Muhamed's desert night* and some significant words 'desert', 'goat', 'camel' written in a language related to the story (Berber language or Arabic). The example on the left shows how Redouane, a bilingual adult, helped children to produce some passages and words from the story in Arabic. He also provided a transliteration in Roman script so that the children could recite the Arabic text.

Children should be encouraged to illustrate the book carefully to reflect the cultural setting that is depicted in the story. The pages could be numbered using Arabic numerals.

Working in pairs, children could follow this learning activity by selecting and using other texts from a range of cultures. Children could be encouraged to transport a familiar story to a different country or cultural context or region using their own knowledge of these different settings, for example, transporting a story from London to Glasgow, England to Ghana or St Lucia or Jamaica and vice versa. The story can be reconstructed using appropriate cultural artefacts and including a few expressions or phrases in the new language or culture. Children can make their own storybooks using these ideas.

MULTILINGUAL STORIES AND DEVELOPING STORY CONCEPT

Hilary Hester (1983) uses Vladimir Propp's analysis of story structures in terms of 'moves'. In the examples she gives of a Bengali story *'The old woman and the rice thief'* and an Iranian folk tale *'Mr Friend and Mr Foe'*, the 'moves' relate to a negative act or thought followed by a series of attempts to rectify the damage leading to a final resolution. Traditional tales from many different cultures can be analysed in this way. Below is the first page of *The boogey man's wife*, a Liberian traditional tale from the Mano tribe (Aardema and Ruffins 1995) which uses the same sequence of 'moves'.

In the old days, in Mano households in Liberia, children were taught strict obedience to their parents. And when daughters married, they were expected to obey their husbands.

But when young and beautiful Goma was given to the old and ugly Boogey Man – in exchange for a night's lodging! – there was trouble ahead.
In those days, the only roads in the jungle were paths made by elephants. People walked to market on the elephants' paths ...

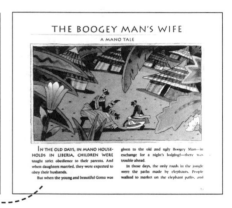

Children find it interesting and cognitively challenging to identify the 'moves' in stories they know and this in turn helps them to structure their own ideas for stories. This activity should be accompanied by a discussion of cultural similarities and differences and ways of expressing ideas as suggested in the activities above so that it is not abstracted from a focus on the meanings in the stories.

Hester (1983) also mentions some common themes which appear in stories across cultures. She lists some typical examples arising from people's common preoccupations and anxieties in all cultures:

> *'the nature of the supernatural and the power of gods over people; origins of the earth; monsters; animals as helpers of people; difficult tasks set to test the power and skills of individuals; wicked step-parents and orphaned children; contrasts between rich and poor, good and evil, beautiful and ugly; conflicts between*

young and old, male and female; transfiguration into new garments, new appearances, new buildings; the journey as a symbol for self discovery and resolution ...'

There are numerous stories from different cultures on the themes listed above which teachers can use as examples to draw out children's own knowledge of stories from their families or communities. Parents or other adults can be usefully involved in this.

This chapter shows how metalinguistic concepts, such as those in the National Literacy Strategy, can be taught through stories in ways that make sense to children. The use of stories across cultures develops a deeper knowledge and understanding about language, culture and identity. It develops children's awareness of how language is used in stories and the relationship between story structure, setting and events. Stories provide an approach to language learning that involves fun, imagination and collaboration. In the next chapter we discuss language work based on words, phrases and sentences.

4. Words, phrases and sentences

This chapter aims to:

- show the importance of working with words, phrases and sentences in a variety of languages;

- provide a range of teaching approaches which introduce words, phrases and sentence structures in different languages;

- reinforce the metalinguistic concepts featured in the National Literacy Strategy by learning and using different languages;

- show how skills and concepts are transferable between languages;

- play with words and sentence patterns in different languages and have fun.

THE IMPORTANCE OF WORD AND SENTENCE LEVEL WORK ACROSS LANGUAGES

The National Literacy Strategy calls for teachers to work at word, sentence and text level in developing pupils' literacy and understanding of how language is used to construct meaning. With support from the strategy materials and training, teachers are now developing a wealth of approaches to these three levels in Standard English. Many of these activities could also be related to any other language or to other varieties of English. This would strengthen language learning in English and enable children to transfer skills and concepts between languages. It shows children that the underlying principles of how language works are the same in all languages. This creates a positive curiosity and motivates children to learn another language. It also helps to raise the self-esteem of those whose identities are closely tied to being speakers of other languages or different varieties of English. In the statement below the author reflects on how knowing three languages as a child supported her literacy development.

My mother taught me, … to read and write in Bengali, Hindi and English at home, almost simultaneously. [She] … taught me to decode text in Bengali very early using phonic skills … Reading in Bengali made sense to me as I spoke Bengali at home … My mother used the same processes and principles … to teach me Hindi … The story of my learning to read in English (which was my third language at this stage) may look quite simple at one level. Learning the alphabet followed a sing-song pattern of vowel practice, for example, the cat sat on the mat *to decode simple words. My mother used the same method of teaching me the grapho-phonic principles in English as she had in Bengali and Hindi …*

By this time I had developed a strong concept about how the written language works and the arbitrariness of the naming system in language or that language is a rule governed system. ... I would say there was a fluid interchange of knowledge, concepts and skills between my three languages to develop early literacy in Bengali, Hindi and English ...

(Datta 2000: 3)

The understanding of language as a symbolic representation is an important conceptual leap that is fundamental to literacy. This conceptual understanding can be supported by the realisation that meanings can be communicated in different ways using different languages and language varieties. An openness to the sounds of other languages, such as demonstrated by Jessica in Chapter 1, makes all children potential language learners. Children can benefit from exposure to written and spoken forms in different languages. Four year-old Charlotte, for example, is a monolingual English-speaking child from North London. In her nursery reading room she chose to read a dual-language book in English and Vietnamese called *Farmer duck* (Waddell and Oxenbury 1993), a story which had been read to her frequently. She started reading the English text confidently by using her memory of the rhythm of the text and when asked, was able to identify the repeated words such as 'quack', 'duck', 'moo', 'cow' and some phrase patterns in the text, for example 'How goes the work?'

Half way through Charlotte's reading, the adult observing her asked if she could read the other text (in Vietnamese). The immediate response was 'Yes, I know some of this language' and she began fingering the Vietnamese text making small and varied sounds with tone and intonation which imitated the rhythms of sounds that she heard in different languages in the nursery. Although not uttering any recognisable words, she showed a developing metalinguistic skill in the ability to step outside her language and imitate what she thinks are the sounds of Vietnamese. She asked her teacher to identify for her the Vietnamese words for 'quack', 'duck', etc, in the text. In so doing, Charlotte was transferring her understanding of word boundaries and word shapes in a written text from English to Vietnamese, thereby shaping her own metalinguistic understanding.

Thus, explicit opportunities to meet the sounds, words and sentences of other languages presented in school from the earliest age help to develop learners' holistic (academic) knowledge about language. It is also a valuable and stimulating experience for children to learn that there are links and similarities between languages and to compare words and sentences in a range of languages. Some of the language aspects studied in English such as word classes (nouns, verbs, adjectives, adverbs, prepositions), punctuation, syllables, etc, can usefully be compared with the structures of other languages. Rhymes, rhythms and patterns in other languages as well as English can help children to realise and appreciate phonetic and structural patterns and thus increase their phonological awareness.

Words in the classroom

When learning a foreign language the learner usually begins with either individual words or language 'chunks' representing single functions. Thus working at word level in a range of languages is a valuable entry into the business of learning other languages.

There are a number of ways in which words in different languages can be brought in to the primary classroom. Teachers may wish to focus on a particular language or variety for a period of time, for example, if the teacher is bilingual and shares his or her language with the class. Sometimes an older child or an adult with a connection to a particular language is available to help (e.g. a student teacher, a teaching assistant, parent or governor). Alternatively a particular topic may relate well to a specific language, for example the study of deserts while reading *Muhamed's desert night* (see Chapter 3) could include learning words associated with desert life in a Berber language or in Arabic. Another example comes from a teacher in North London, who taught her class of seven-year-olds the Swahili names for some of the animals in a unit of work entitled 'Animal Stories'. Working on the story, *The lion king* she encouraged the children to learn some Swahili words and phrases such as *'hakuna matata'* (no worries) and *'rafiki'* (friend), and added further words and phrases, which occur in the story, in Swahili which she had learned from her extended family.

Teachers can also use a variety of languages and build up a repertoire of resources to create a multilingual environment and approach to all their work. The list of suggestions below provides a starting point. Bringing words from other languages can be a challenge for teachers who are monolingual themselves or work where there is less linguistic diversity among the population; however, there are resources available – both human and in the form of materials as well as websites. The references at the end of this book include some examples of books that can be used to support these activities.

NACELL (the National Advisory Centre on Early Language Learning) is an invaluable further source of support – see **www.nacell.org.uk.**

Displays

Classrooms usually contain attractive interactive displays of all kinds in order to support learning, show recognition of pupils' achievements, give information and label equipment. Making displays in a range of languages provides a rich and interactive multilingual environment. These could include displays of:

- photocopied pages from the European Language Portfolio showing the range of language knowledge of the class, with examples of words in each language, or children can design their own displays;
- a map of the world showing where the languages listed in the A–Z survey (see Chapter 1) are predominantly spoken, each one written in the appropriate language;
- a map showing journeys of languages from countries of origin of pupils, parents, school staff, neighbours and visitors;

- a welcome sign greeting people in many languages on the door (such as the greeting poem in Chapter 1);
- word sets such as numbers, days of the week, months, colours, greetings etc, in a range of languages;
- word class sets – nouns, verbs, adjectives, adverbs, prepositions – in different languages;
- labels on classroom furniture and equipment in different languages;
- an ongoing display of cultural items or artefacts labelled in different languages.

It is important that such displays are interactively used in children's learning and not merely tokenistic.

SUGGESTIONS FOR USING DISPLAYS

DAYS OF THE WEEK

A display of days of the week in different languages, for example, could lead to an investigation of stories, myths or poems associated with days of the week in different cultures. In Indo-European languages days of the week are named after planets or heavenly bodies, which in turn are often linked to mythological stories. For example *Sunday* in English and *robibar* in Bengali both refer to the sun (*robi* = sun, *bar* = day in Bengali). Similarly *mardi* in French, *martes* in Spanish and *mongolbar* in Bengali all rcfcr to the planet and god *Mars*. Children could make a quilt or pattern display of the stories.

All the days have special significance for Hindus. For example, Thursday, or *Brihoshpotibar* in Bengali (or *Brihaspativar* in Hindi) is associated with the planet Jupiter, and in Hinduism it is dedicated to the goddess Laxmi, signifying family prosperity and happiness. The example below shows thirteen-year-old Hindi-speaking Parul's image of the goddess Laxmi, especially worshipped on Brihspativar, and her personal relationship with its significance in Hindu tradition. This is what Parul wrote about the goddess Laxmi:

Parul

This is the picture of the Hindu goddess Laxmi. Laxmi is the goddess of wealth and happiness in the family. My mother like most Hindus worships her and fasts on Brihaspativar (Thursday) to show respect to goddess Laxmi and receive her blessings. During Diwali, Hindus light small lamps called diya *to welcome Laxmi into their homes – the idea is to welcome light over darkness. Most Hindu goddesses have more than two arms to symbolise strength.*

Everyday exchanges

Many teachers in schools in London use greetings in different languages when calling the morning register. A teacher at a school in North London plans collaboratively with her class to use different languages every week for the morning and afternoon register. The class chooses the language for the week and finds out how to greet people and ask how they are (or some other common expressions) in that particular language. This can sometimes lead to further explorations of the words used, for example noticing that *bonjour* (French), *bom dia* (Portuguese), *bongiorno* (Italian), *buenas dias* (Spanish) all start with a similar sounding word for 'good' which comes from the Latin adjective *bonum* = good. Posing the question 'why?' can then lead to historical investigations about the influence of the Romans on European language and culture and the reasons for this influence (see Chapter 6).

Other greetings in different languages for different occasions such as birthdays or religious or secular festivals can lead to similar investigations into links between languages and the history of the peoples associated with them, for example, *eid mubarak* for the Muslim festival at the end of Ramadan. Different levels of formality in different languages might also arise as a topic of discussion, which can pave the way for understanding different uses and registers of language for different audiences. For example, Namita and Nirmala (in Chapter 1) know that they have to say '*namaste*' or '*aap kaise hain?*' (how are you?) as a mark of respect when greeting Hindi-speaking adults rather than 'hi' or 'hello' which they might use for their peers.

Word games

Children enjoy word games of all kinds. You could play the alphabet game: children stand in a circle and think of the name of an object in any language which begins with the same letter or sound as their first name. For example, in French: *Je m'appelle Cathy la cathédrale*. They then have to remember the names and the objects of their neighbours to the left and right, for example, Karim – *kaula* (= 'banana' in Bengali), Terry – *el toro* (= 'bull' in Spanish) and so on. Each word can also be accompanied by a
mime to help children remember them (e.g. putting hands together as if in prayer and then lifting them up high above the head for *la cathédrale*, peeling a banana for *kaula*, putting fingers up on the head and butting to show *el toro,* etc.). A display on the wall showing nouns in different languages could act as a prompt for this game.

Word journeys

The map below shows how the word for the spice 'ginger' has travelled across the world. This shows links between languages, showing historical migrations, trade and invasions, which have brought the spice and the word for it from one part of the world to another.

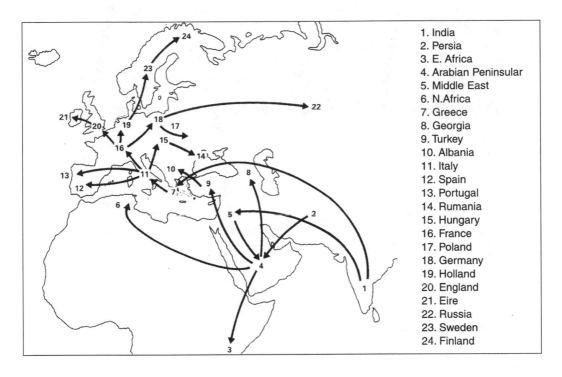

| 1. India |
| 2. Persia |
| 3. E. Africa |
| 4. Arabian Peninsular |
| 5. Middle East |
| 6. N.Africa |
| 7. Greece |
| 8. Georgia |
| 9. Turkey |
| 10. Albania |
| 11. Italy |
| 12. Spain |
| 13. Portugal |
| 14. Rumania |
| 15. Hungary |
| 16. France |
| 17. Poland |
| 18. Germany |
| 19. Holland |
| 20. England |
| 21. Eire |
| 22. Russia |
| 23. Sweden |
| 24. Finland |

Words for different foods often travel in this way, for example a sweet known as *Halva* in Turkish, Greek, Arabic and English is called *Halwa* in India (see Chapter 5).

Numbers in different languages

If someone in the class knows how to count from 1–10 or 1–5 in a different language, he or she can teach the others. When there are several children with knowledge of different languages in the class they can teach a small group to chant or sing the numbers, accompanied perhaps by a mime or dance and then each group can perform their chant, song and/or dance and teach the rest of the class. A class can make a frieze showing numbers 1–10 in a range of different languages. This can then be used to find similarities between languages, as in the examples from different language families shown left and below.

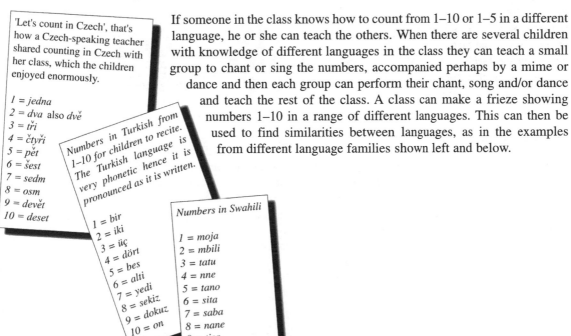

'Let's count in Czech', that's how a Czech-speaking teacher shared counting in Czech with her class, which the children enjoyed enormously.

1 = jedna
2 = dva also dvě
3 = tři
4 = čtyři
5 = pět
6 = šest
7 = sedm
8 = osm
9 = devět
10 = deset

Numbers in Turkish from 1–10 for children to recite. The Turkish language is very phonetic hence it is pronounced as it is written.

1 = bir
2 = iki
3 = üç
4 = dört
5 = bes
6 = alti
7 = yedi
8 = sekiz
9 = dokuz
10 = on

Numbers in Swahili

1 = moja
2 = mbili
3 = tatu
4 = nne
5 = tano
6 = sita
7 = saba
8 = nane
9 = tisa
10 = kumi

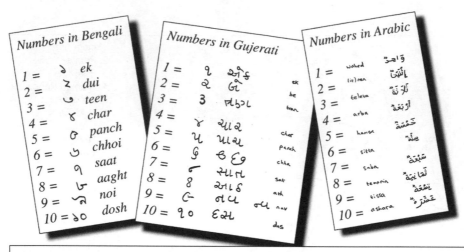

Numbers in Bengali

1 = ১ ek
2 = ২ dui
3 = ৩ teen
4 = ৪ char
5 = ৫ panch
6 = ৬ chhoi
7 = ৭ saat
8 = ৮ aaght
9 = ৯ noi
10 = ১০ dosh

Numbers in Gujerati

1 = ૧ ... ek
2 = ૨ ... be
3 = ૩ ... tran
4 = ૪ ...
5 = ૫ ... char
6 = ૬ ... panch
7 = ૭ ... chha
8 = ૮ ... sat
9 = ૯ ... ath ... nav
10 = ૧૦ ... das

Numbers in Arabic

1 = wahed
2 = (it)nen
3 = teleta
4 = arba
5 = hamse
6 = sitta
7 = saba
8 = temenin
9 = tissa
10 = ashara

Examples of mathematical operations and terminology in Turkish:

Toplama	çikarma	bölme	çarpma
addition	subtraction	division	multiplication
24 + 56 = 80	48 - 14 = 34	64 ، 2 = 32	16 x 4 = 64

A Bengali-speaking teacher taught her class of eight year-olds how to count to ten in Bengali. They enjoyed it so much they wanted to learn to say 20, 30, 40, etc, so that they could use a range of bigger numbers. Stuart, one of the boys in the class, later presented the teacher with a page of sums that he gave himself to do using Bengali numerals.

Sums using Bengali numerals

Personal sentences

The examples below show a display of children writing a few personal sentences about themselves in a different language. Young Pathfinder 9: *The literacy link* (Cheater and Farren 2001) shows a similar activity in French, Spanish and German. Children can use the display to find out how to say simple sentences such as 'How are you?', 'My name is …' , 'I speak …', etc, in various languages.

Portuguese example:

Olá, como é que te chamas?
Hello, what's your name?

O meu nome é Sebastian. Eu tenho seis anos de idade.
My name is Sebastian. I am six years old.

Sebastian

Eu vivo em Londres com a minha mãe e o meu pai e eu tenho muitos amigos.
I live in London with my mummy and daddy and I have lots of friends.

Eu falo Português e Inglés e um pouco de Espanhol com a minha mãe e pai.
I speak Portuguese, English and a bit of Spanish with my mum and dad.

Quando eu vou à Portugal de férias eu falo Português com a minha avó e avo e com os meus tios e tias.
When I go to Portugal in holidays I speak Portuguese with my grandparents and my uncles and aunties.

Quando eu vou ao Chile de férias eu falo Espanhol com a minha outra familia
When I go to Chile I speak Spanish with my other family.

Eu tenho muitos primos. Alguns vivem em Portugal e outros no Chile.
I have lots of cousins. Some live in Portugal and some live in Chile.

Eu gosto muito de brincar e ir à praia com os meus primos.
I love to play with my cousins and go to the seaside with them.

A minha comida favorite é peixe com batatas fritas.
My favourite food is fish and chips.

Eu gosto de jugar futebol e nadar.
I enjoy playing football and swimming.

O meu passatempo predilécto é ajudar a minha mãe no jardim, andar de bicicleta no parque e ouvir histórias que a minha mãe e pai me contam.
My favourite hobby is helping my mum in the garden, cycling in the park and listening to stories that my mummy and daddy tell me.

Greek example:

Γεια σου.
Yiasou.
Hello!

Με λενε Λεωνιδα.
Me lene Leonitha.
My name is Leonidas.

Μιλω Ελληνικα και Αγγλικα.
Milo Ellinika ke Anglika.
I speak Greek and English.

Leonidas

Μενω στην Αγγλια.
Meno stin Anglia.
I live in England.

Πηγαινω στο Ελληνικο σχολειο το Σαββατο.
Biyeno Elliniko skolio to savato.
I go to Greek school on Saturday.

Παω στην Ελλαδα και στην Κυπρο για διακοπες.
Pao stin Elatha ke stinkypro yia thiakobes.
I go to Greece and Cyprus on holiday.

Εχω 16 εξαδελφια.
Eho 16 exathelfia.
I have 16 cousins.

14 στην Αγγλια.
14 stin Anglia.
14 in England.

2 στην Ελλαδα.
2 stin Elatha.
2 in Greece.

Μου αρεσουνοι πατατες, τα λουκανικα και κοτοπουλο ναγγετς.
Mou aresoun e patates, ta loukanika ke kotopoulo nuyets.
I like potatoes, sausages and chicken nuggets.

Μου αρεσει να παιζω ποδοσφαιρο και να κολυμπαω πολυ γρηγορα.
Mou aresi na pezo ke na kolibao boli yriyora.
I like playing football and swimming very quickly.

Μου αρεσει να κανω ποδηλατο στο παρκο.
Mou aresi na kano bothilato sto parko.
I like riding my bike at the park.

Μαθαινω να παιζω κιθαρα.
Matheno na pezo tin githara.
I am learning to play the guitar.

Japanese example:

Konnichiwa.
Hello.
こんにちは。

Boku no namae wa Yuuki desu.
My name is Yuki.
僕の名前は裕貴です。

Yuki

Boku wa jyuissai desu.
I am eleven years old.
僕は 11 才です。

Boku wa baiorin wo hikimasu.
I play the violin.
僕はバイオリンを弾きます。

Otonani nattara uchuhikoshi ka kenchikuka ka konpyuutagem no dezain a ni naritai desu.
When I grow up I want to be an astronaut or an architect or a computer game designer.
大人になったら，宇宙飛行士か建築家かコンピュータゲームのデザイナーになりたいです。

Tokui na kamoku wa sansuu to onngaku desu.
I am good at maths and music.
得意な科目は算数と音楽です。

Watashi no namae wa Risa desu.
My name is Lisa.
私の名前は理紗です。

Watashi wa nana sai desu.
I am seven years old.
私は 7 才です。

Watashi wa baree to baiorin to piano wo naratteimasu.
I have lessons in ballet, violin and piano.
私はバレエとバイオリンとピアノを習っています。

Lisa

Watashi wa baree ga ichiban suki desu.
I like ballet best.
私はバレエが一番好きです。

Sukina tabemono wa robusuta to inariz ushi desu.
My favourite foods are lobster and in arizushi.
好きな食べ物はロブスターといなりずしです。

Watashi wa mekyabetu ga kirai desu.
I hate Brussels sprouts.
私は芽キャベツが嫌いです。

Sayonara.
Good bye.
さようなら。

SINKING AND FLOATING

If a suitable adult (bilingual teacher, teaching assistant, student teacher, etc) with knowledge of another language can be found, a science lesson on sinking and floating is a good way to teach some individual words and phrases in another language. 'Sinking and floating' is a typical science activity designed to discuss properties of different materials and to demonstrate the methodology of a simple scientific enquiry. It is likely to be a very familiar activity to most primary teachers and it is suggested that a teacher rather than a non-teaching adult is used for this lesson as it does require teaching and miming skill to conduct it successfully. The activity is very visual and procedural and therefore it is possible to do it in any language. The linguistic focus is on naming objects plus two simple verbal phrases and questions. Below is an example of a teacher using Hindi for this activity:

The class worked in groups of four or five children at each table. On each table was a tank of water and six objects, e.g. a pencil, a cork, a banana, a spoon, a piece of paper, a stone. The teacher had her own tank and set of objects. She used a feather and a coin to demonstrate, asking in Hindi with a lot of mime to support meaning:

Will it sink? (Dubegi?)
Will it float? (Taregi?)
(No English was used by the teacher throughout the lesson.)

She then entered the Hindi words for 'coin' and 'feather' in the appropriate column (sinking or floating) on a chart.

'Dubegi?'	'Taregi?'
Paisa	Pankh

The teacher then held up and repeated the Hindi words for the other six objects, getting the children to repeat them, as well as the word for water 'pani'. Repetition and playing with the sounds of the words helps children to remember them. This can be made fun by using different dynamics of voice (loud/soft), or different speeds (starting slow then gradually speeding up). The teacher kept repeating the question 'Ye kya hai?' (What is this?), and if the children replied in English, she said 'Hindi mei iska nam kya hai?' (What is it called in Hindi?) While they were repeating, the teacher wrote the words on the whiteboard in Hindi script and transliterated in Roman script for the children to repeat and rehearse. She also drew each object on a sheet on the wall to support learning. The teacher then asked the class whether they thought the object will sink (dubegi?) or float (taregi?) and wrote the children's predictions on a chart in the appropriate column. The children then carried out their own tests and recorded the results by ticking or crossing in the appropriate column. Alternatively the children can draw the objects in the appropriate columns. Inevitably they will use their first language when they work in groups as this will help them to think, make sense of the new language, reflect on what is happening as well as transfer their skills and conceptual understanding. It is important to allow them to do this as the language learner's knowledge about the first language helps make connections with the learning of other languages. It also helps the learner to be at ease in a context where an unfamiliar language is used so that this experience becomes positive and enjoyable rather than stressful.

The activities in this chapter show how word and sentence level work carried out in languages other than English strengthens children's knowledge and understanding about how language works and helps them to stand back from their own language and think about language at an abstract and academic level. The enjoyment of these activities provides an excellent motivation and preparation for learning new languages in the future. In the next chapter, 'Doing language', there are further ideas for active and enactive language learning.

5. Doing language

This chapter aims to:

- provide ideas for fun activities that will motivate children to enjoy learning language;

- enable children to experience collaborative language learning;

- encourage language learning activities in English and other languages;

- provide ideas for further activities which enable teachers to work in partnership with speakers of other languages.

Children in all cultures learn language by doing things co-operatively and collaboratively. This chapter provides ideas for fun activities in which children will enjoy learning a new language.

 ## DRAMA ACTIVITIES

Drama activities can be based on popular texts with rhythmic grouping of words, for example *We're going on a bear hunt* by Michael Rosen. The story describes the hunters (children) going through different terrain to find the bear. It is an excellent story for teaching the concepts of prepositions and interesting adjectives which bring the story alive.

For example, when the 'hunters' get to the long wavy grass they say:

We can't go over it.
We can't go under it.
Oh no!
We've got to go through it!

They repeat the above refrain when they come to a deep, cold river, then to thick, oozy mud, a big, dark forest, a swirling, whirling snowstorm and a narrow, gloomy cave where they finally meet:

One shiny, wet nose!
Two big furry ears!
Two big goggly eyes!
IT'S A BEAR!!!!

and then go running back home through each terrain again.

The teacher should first act out the story with the narrative of the text in English, encouraging the children to join in the sequence of actions. The story is then repeated in another language for children to respond to the 'tune' of the new language and act out the story sequence again. The essence of this activity is for children to gain a sensual experience of the phonetics and rhythm of another language by enacting the story. For this reason the version in another language should not be expected to be a direct translation as language expressions vary across cultures. The adjectives, for example, could be chosen for their humour, sound or rhythm to go with the narrative sequence. The teacher and children's role play in both languages should emphasise the prepositional phrases and adjectives. The teacher can then use the gestures to make lists of prepositions and adjectives in both languages.

Another popular children's story, *Handa's surprise* by Eileen Browne, lends itself to a different kind of role play and language learning experience, this time in a tropical setting. In this story Handa decides to take a basketful of tropical fruits carried on her head to her friend in a neighbouring village. However, on the way different animals steal the fruit (the monkey steals the banana, the ostrich steals the guava, the zebra steals the orange, the elephant steals the mango, the giraffe steals the pineapple, the parrot steals the passion fruit) until the basket is nearly empty. But as she passes under an orange tree an enormous goat butts against the tree trunk and shakes all the oranges off the tree and into her basket. Handa's surprise occurs when her friend greets her and exclaims at the lovely oranges in her basket. This story offers extension of vocabulary (fruits, animals) in different languages as well as enacting Handa's walk to her friend. Wearing traditional cultural clothes and artefacts

Will she like the round juicy orange ...

(headgear, beads, etc) adds to the enrichment of the language learning experience. A student teacher worked with the story in English and Somali with seven-to-nine year-old children in a London school. With the help of Somali-speaking children she produced the following bilingual word banks.

ANIMALS

English	Somali
monkey	*daayeer*
ostrich	*gorayo*
zebra	*dameer-dibadeed*
elephant	*maroodi*

FRUITS

English	Somali
banana	*muus*
guava	*saytuun*
mango	*mange*
orange	*Llin macaan*

Here is a word bank of the animal and fruit names in Arabic produced by an Arabic-speaking adult:

English	Arabic	Arabic words in Roman script
monkey	قرد	*alkerdo* (stress on *k*)
ostrich	نعامة	*annama* (stress on *an*)
zebra	فيل	*himar wachee* (aspirated strongly with a puff of air)
elephant	الفيل	*al feelle* (stress on *lle*)
giraffe	زرافة	*azzarafa* (stress on *rafa*)
antelope	ظبي	*addabio* (stress on *ad*)
parrot	ببغاء	*Babaka* (stress on *ka*; *k* is guttural)
goat	معزة	*al maiza* (stress on *za*)
banana	موز	*al mozo*
guava	جوافة	*al jawfa*
orange	برتقال	*al bortokal*
mango	ألمانكا	*annanass*
avocado	أبوكادو	*abokado*

Kate, an Ibo-speaking teacher student, transformed *Handa's surprise* into the song below for her class. Although she wrote the song in English, the tune, rhythm and the pattern with use of a refrain related to her own African culture.

Handa took some beautiful fruits for her friend Akeyo
What was Handa's surprise?
The monkey took the yellow banana
What was Handa's surprise?
The ostrich took the sweet-smelling guava
What was Handa's surprise?
The zebra took the nice juicy orange
What was Handa's surprise?
The elephant took the red ripe mango
What was Handa's surprise?
The giraffe took the green avocado
What was Handa's surprise?
The parrot took the purple passion fruit
What was Handa's surprise?
The goat crashed into the orange tree
Many oranges fell for all to see
That was Handa's surprise!

Action songs and rhymes have always been a popular resource to tune into the phonology and the syntax of the new language in a fun way. Some poems and rhymes also lend themselves to dramatic interpretations, such as the Czech poem below:

Jiří áček – Pro slepičí kvoč

Říkadlo pro lidoopy

Hopsa, hejsa,
hop, hop, hop,
takhle skáče lidoop.
Hopsa hejsa,
po pralese,
až se celá země třese.
Hopsa, hejsa,
hop, hop, hop,
ještě že tam není strop.

A poem for an ape

Hopsa, hejsa,
Hop, hop, hop,
An ape skips like that.
Hopsa, hejsa,
In a rainforest,
All the ground is quaking.
Hopsa hejsa,
Hop, hop hop,
It's good there's no ceiling!

ACTION AND RHYTHM

The repetitive nature of many activities in the nursery setting lends itself to repetitive and rhythmic use of language. For example, playing with dough the teacher leads a chant as follows:

Squeeze, squeeze, squeeze the dough,
Squash, squash, squash the dough,
Pat, pat, pat the dough,
Pinch, pinch, pinch the dough,
Roll, roll, roll the dough,
Roll it hard, harder, harder,
Look I've made a … (star, chapati, simit)!

(Datta 2000: 239)

A chant such as this can be conducted in any language to accompany the actions. In doing so children can have fun as they 'tune into' the sounds and rhythms of another language. Here is a Turkish version of the same chant:

Sık sık sık hamuru sık
Bastır bastır bastır hamuru bastır
Vur vur vur hamura vur
Yuvarla yuvarla yuvarla hamuru yuvarla
Yuvarla yuvarla daha fazla yuvarla
Bak ben bir yııdız yaptım … Bir simit!

Actions and words linked to play with water, sand or construction toys can be used in the same way.

SONGS

Every language has counting songs, and some of these can be action songs as well. Teachers can make a collection of these songs on tape to teach numbers in different languages. The example below is in Czech. The English translation is also provided so that teachers can familiarise pupils with the content. As you can see, some of the humour generated by the repetition of the rhyme in the Czech poem is lost in the English translation; the inclusion of 'grandfather' in the song is more understandable if you look at the sound patterns in Czech.

Sluníčko Sedmitecné	**A seven dot ladybird**
Jedna tečka, druhá tečka	First dot, second dot
Vítek čeká na dědečka.	Vitek is waiting for grandfather.
Třetí, čtvrtá, pátá	Third, fourth, fifth
leť, beruško zlatá!	Fly, golden ladybird!
Šestá tečka, sedmá tečka	Sixth dot, seventh dot
Lítej, broučku do kolečka!	Fly, beetle all around!

František Hrubín

Young Pathfinder 6: *Let's join in: Rhymes, poems and songs* (Cynthia Martin and Catherine Cheater 1998) gives a number of examples of counting and other action songs.

The song 'Head, shoulders, knees and toes' provides some energetic action and can be sung in many different languages to teach children the words for parts of the body in the language. The children can enjoy touching the relevant parts of the body as they sing the words for them. The fun is increased if you miss out the words, giving the actions only for one line at a time or if you sing and do the actions at different speeds. Below is a French version of this action song:

> *Tête, épaules, genoux, pieds,*
> *Genoux, pieds.*
> *Tête, épaules, genoux, pieds,*
> *Genoux, pieds.*
> *Les yeux, le nez,*
> *La bouche, les oreilles,*
> *Tête, épaules, genoux, pieds,*
> *Genoux, pieds.*

 ## GAMES

Games provide a very useful way of learning another language as they allow for taking turns and the use of repetitive words, phrases or sentences. They encourage friendly competition and collaboration in effective language use. Children feel comfortable with the rituals of familiar games and can transfer these to new games in new languages.

Board games provide familiar structures which can be adapted to different language learning needs. A multilingual board game can be constructed with different coloured task cards which match coloured squares on the board. On landing on a pink square, for example, the player takes a pink card and then prepares with a partner or 'team' to carry out the task described on the first pink card in the pile. Examples of tasks are:

- Count to five in any language.
- Greet your friend in any language.
- Sing a song or recite a poem in any language.
- Name a food or dish in any language.
- Name two languages spoken in India.
- Which languages are spoken in these countries (select one)?: Venezuela, Brazil, Kenya, Nigeria, Malaysia, Iceland.
- Name five community languages spoken in Britain.
- Say a verb in any language and mime it (e.g. *aao* in Hindi = come).
- Identify this language (example of words, sentence or poem in another language).

Points can be awarded for completion of the tasks and extra points for additional examples or information.

A key aim of this game is to promote discussion about language in which children share their language knowledge. The tasks can relate to specific language topics or vocabulary recently covered in class. Children could also devise their own set of cards based on their own ideas and knowledge of languages.

Classroom games such as 'Simon says' can be played in any language and can teach children vocabulary and metalinguistic concepts such as:

- imperatives – (stand up, sit down, sing a song);
- parts of the body – (touch your nose, touch your toes);
- adverbs – (walk slowly, talk loudly);
- prepositions – (put your hand on your head, crouch under the table);
- naming of objects in the classroom – (pick up a book, point to a pair of scissors).

If children in the class know different languages they could take the lead in teaching and demonstrating these instructions in their language.

COOKING

Cooking is a good activity for 'doing language' – children enjoy the activity and the product and can learn language and become aware of cultures at the same time. It is interesting to note that 'stew' cooked in different ways has the same underlying principles in all cultures. Whatever seasonal vegetables are available are washed and chopped, sometimes adding meat or fish and are cooked over a period of time to satisfy everyone's taste and appetite. The children could be encouraged to find out the ingredients and how to cook their favourite stew (goulash, curry, ragout, stifado ...). They could then talk about how different cuisines have travelled from the countries of origin to Britain.

Following a recipe in another language involves understanding imperatives, expressions of quantity and time, and extension of vocabulary to name ingredients. Like the 'sinking and floating' science activity described in Chapter 4, it is a very visual and sequential activity with built-in repetition of verbs and nouns that helps language learning in a structured way.

On the next page we have an example of making *Suji Halwa* (Semolina Halwa) the Indian way. The recipe was written by Parul and her mother Kalpana Agrawal.

बनाने की विधि

पहले कढ़ाई मे २०० ग्राम घी धीमी आँच मे गरम कीरेये,

जैसे ही घी पिघल जाये उसमे २५० ग्राम सूजी डाल
दे, इसे धीमी आँच मे लगातार चलाते रहे,

अब १½ पाइंट पानी उबाल कर उसमे २०० ग्राम
चीनी डाल दे और चीनी का घोल बनाइये,

जब सूजी का रंग सुनहला पड़ने लगे तब
इसमे चीनी का घोल डाले, धीमी आँच मे
इसे लगातार चलाते रहे, जब सारी सूजी
सोख जाये उसमे एक कप ठंडा दूध डालिये
और लगातार चलाते रहे, जब दूध सोख
जाये, इसे उतार ले

इच्छानुसार आप मेवा काटकर डाल सकते है,
अब गर्म गर्म मे हलवा खाइये!

Method

First, heat 200 grams of ghee (clarified butter) in low heat.

When the ghee melts put 250 grams of semolina. Cook in low heat stirring continuously.

Boil one and a half-pint of water. Add 250 grams of sugar to make syrup.

When the semolina turns golden brown pour the syrup and cook in low heat stirring continuously.

When the syrup is absorbed in the semolina, add a cup of cold milk. Keep on stirring until milk is absorbed.

If you like you can put chopped almonds or pistachio in it. Enjoy eating your halwa!

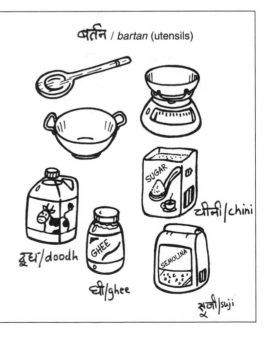

बर्तन / bartan (utensils)

दूध / doodh
घी / ghee
चीनी / chini
सूजी / suji

And below is the Turkish way of making Halva. The recipe was supplied by Pembe Issa.

Türk Helvasi *(Turkish Halva)*

Malzemeler

3 çay bardağı simit
yarim çay bardağı fistik yağı
1 çay bardağı badem içi
3 çay bardağı şeker
6 çay bardağı su

Metod
Tencere içine 6 çay bardağı su, 3 su bardağı şeker, biraz gül suyu kaynamaya bırakilir. Diğer taraftan başka bir kapta yarim çay bardagı fistik yağı içinde daha önceden kaynanmıs badem içleri dökülür ve kavrulur. Pembelenince simit kısık ateşle tahta kaşıkla pembeleninceye kadar devamlı olarak kavrulur. Simit pembelenince kaynar şerbet dökülür ve su çekinceye kadar karıştırılır sonra ateşten indirilir. Tepsiye dökülür. Soğuyunca üzerine bahar serpilir ve kesilir.

Turkish Halva in English

Ingredients
3 teaspoons of semolina
half a glass of cooking oil
1 glassful boiled almonds (take off skins)
3 glassfuls of sugar
6 glassfuls of water
a quarter glassful of rosewater

Method
Pour 6 glassfuls of water, sugar and rose water in a pan and let it boil slowly. Put half a glass of cooking oil in another pan. Pour semolina and already boiled almonds into it letting them cook slowly. Keep stirring slowly until the semolina starts turning pink. When this happens pour the contents of the first pan (rosewater, water and sugar – now can be called 'sherbet') into the pan with semolina. Keep stirring until the sherbet is fully absorbed. Turn the cooker off and let it cool. Finally cut into fine portions to serve.

 ## CIRCLE TIME

Circle Time in schools is normally used to create an awareness of each other as people and an awareness of issues that affect children as well as a place to create a context for developing friendships and responsibility towards each other. Because of its human, emotional and personal nature as a learning context, it provides a rich resource for sharing and learning languages.

Children's voices are stronger in the safe and secure environment of Circle Time. A five year-old child named Dipesh initiated a discussion about greetings in Gujerati in response to his teacher's suggestion that the children said 'Good morning' to each other in a different language.

> *'We don't say 'Good morning' in Gujerati.* [There's an equivalent expression in Gujerati but it is very formal.] *We say,* 'Keim chho?', *How are you?*
> 'Saru chhey,' *I'm well.'*
> *And he went on to say,* 'Miss you've got to say,
> 'Dipesh, keim chho?'
> *And I'll say,* 'Saru chhey'.

(Datta 2000: 36–7)

In this exchange Dipesh has drawn on his personal experience to articulate and share an important insight into the relationship between language and culture. Following this exchange the teacher suggested that they choose the way they greet one another in their culture, showing her generosity and respect for the child in acknowledging that teachers can learn from children's knowledge about language and culture.

Another popular activity could be sharing songs and rhymes in different languages. Some teachers have found that this motivates children to go and seek out speakers of other languages to help them learn some rhymes or songs which they can share with peers at circle time. Five year-old Jimmy heard his friends chanting counting rhymes in Panjabi, Greek and Turkish. The following week his teacher was astonished by Jimmy's recitation of a rhyme in Panjabi. Jimmy smiled with pride.

SCRIPTS

Walking around a city almost anywhere in the world, children are likely to come across different scripts used in shop names, street names, newspapers and magazines, places of worship and municipal buildings. The photographs below were taken in different parts of London. They could be used to demonstrate and compare the different scripts used by different languages.

Given below are some samples from children's story books of scripts from different languages. Children can be asked the following questions about them:

- What is your first impression of this writing? Can you describe the shapes of the letters or characters?
- How does it compare with writing in English? Find out the directionality of each script: is it left to right across the page like English? Is it right to left like Arabic or Hebrew scripts? You may know that some languages, like Chinese, are sometimes written from top to bottom. Can you find some of these scripts in the examples below?
- Can you spot capital letters in all the scripts? Can you find different ways of putting full stops?
- Can you spot other punctuation marks? Are they similar to English or different from English?
- What does this tell you about writing in different languages?

In answering these questions children can find out that Bengali and other Asian languages use an alphabet in the same way as English and other European languages, whereas Chinese languages use thousands of different characters to represent words and ideas. Here are some characters that were shared by children in a class where a Chinese speaker took a lead in describing the characters and explaining to his friends how he learns them.

Here is the Bengali alphabet (consonants) with examples of words written in Bengali.

ক	খ	গ	ঘ	ঙ	চ
কলা kola	খেলনা khelna	গরু goru	ঘুড়ি gudhi	রঙ rawng	চা cha
ছ	জ	ঝ	ঞ	ট	ঠ
ছবি chhobee	জগ jog	ঝুড়ি jhuri	মিএও miaow	টিয়া tia	ঠোট thot
ড	ঢ	ণ	ত	থ	দ
ডিম dim	ঢোল dhole	হরিণ horin	তবলা tabla	থালা thala	দাড়ি thari
ধ	ন	প	ফ	ব	ভ
ধনুক donuk	নৌকা nouka	পতাকা potaka	ফুল fool	বল ball	ভাল্লুক bhaalluk
ম	য	র	ল	শ	ষ
মাছ machh	যোগ joug	রসুন roshoon	লেবু laybu	শাড়ী sari	ষাড় shar
স	হ	ড়	ঢ়	য়	ৎ
সাপ shap	হাতি haathee	বুড়ি buri	আষাঢ় ashar	পায়রা payra	কেৎলী ketly
ং	ঃ	ঁ			
সং shong	দুঃখ dukho	চাঁদ chath			

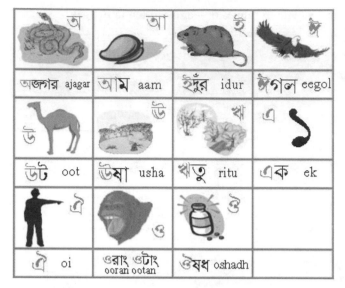

অজগর ajagar	আম aam	ইঁদুর idur	ঈগল eegol
উট oot	ঊষা usha	ঋতু ritu	এক ek
ঐ oi	ওরাং ওটাং ooran ootan	ঔষধ oshadh	

On the left are vowels in Bengali with examples of words using these vowels. It would be an interesting experience for children to try out copying some words, letters or characters in different scripts, to experience and understand that there are many ways of writing and becoming literate. Working with an adult who is literate in the script would be an advantage.

Teachers and children can collect examples of writing in different scripts, including dual language books, food and other wrappings, newspapers, comics and magazines, letters and stamps, coins, etc, to make a collage or a display. They can research to find out more about the script and where it comes from, locating these on a world map in a 'calligraphy corner'.

All of the activities suggested in this chapter involve collaboration between children or children and adults to share language and cultural experiences. They are designed to expand children's personal linguistic knowledge, understanding and experience and inspire interest in language learning. This would also activate children's awareness of the languages around them and stimulate attitude and aptitude for learning languages in the future.

This chapter has used examples from many different languages. In the next chapter we will look at how English is linked to many different languages throughout the world.

6. What is English?

This chapter aims to explore:

- the links between English and other languages and the transfer of knowledge and skills between languages;

- the history of English – deriving from early invasions and contact with many other languages;

- combining use of English with other languages through code-switching and the benefits of this for everyone;

- different ways of using English;

- activities to find out about languages and develop interest in language and learning languages.

The story of the English language is a fascinating one with links to numerous other languages and cultures. It is useful for children to hear this story and understand the links between English and other languages. This raises their awareness of what language is and how it works in all cultures.

The invasions which brought with them the different languages which made up what we now call English provide the first part of this story. The map below shows the direction of invasions by the Angles, Saxons and Jutes (449 AD), the Vikings (800 AD) and the Normans (1066 AD).

Prior to these invasions, Celtic languages similar to modern Irish, Scots Gaelic and Welsh were used predominantly in Britain, with Latin used side by side with these after the Roman invasions of Julius Caesar (55 BC) and the Emperor Claudius (43 AD). Below are some ideas for ways in which teachers can enable children to investigate the influence on English of all the languages associated with these invaders.

A VIKINGS

B ANGLES, SAXONS & JUTES

C NORMANS

PLACE NAMES

Place names in England show the influence of the languages of all these invaders and children enjoy finding out about the origins of the names of places in their local area. The Latin word *castra* meaning 'a camp' has been absorbed into the names of towns occupied by the Romans, as shown in place names ending in -cester or -chester (e.g. Gloucester, Manchester). The name England has derived from the Angles or Angli. Places which include 'thorp' (e.g. Cleethorpes) or ending in -by (Grimsby) were invaded by the Vikings whose language is usually referred to as Old Norse. 'Thorp' comes from the Old Norse for 'village' and '-by' from the word for 'farm' in Old Norse. Of course, the original Celtic languages are also reflected in place names, such as 'tor' (a peak or high rock) in Torquay or 'cumb' (a deep valley) as in Ilfracombe. Children can find out if any of these languages are used in their local place names. A useful reference book for teachers is the *Dictionary of place names in the British Isles* (Room 1988).

Similarly, in many countries place names are associated with the history of the land. For example, in India, Allahabad, Hydrabad or Sikandrabad are associated with the Mughal habitation of these places. The suffix *-abad* (Perso-Arabic) simply means to inhabit. However the place names ending with *-pur* as in Nagpur, Jaipur, Kanpur indicates *nagar* or towns. It is interesting to note that *-pur* in Sanskrit was adapted to anglicised pronunciation *-pore* during British rule. Children should be encouraged to find such common usage of suffixes in place names in different countries and find out what they denote in particular cultures. Locating these places on the map can strengthen such activities and subsequent learning.

ENGLISH AND GERMAN

The languages used by the Angles, Saxons and Jutes were closely related Germanic languages. These powerful invaders imposed their language and wiped out the original Celtic languages except in the extreme north and west. Speakers of English can often understand some German words and phrases because of the connection with the languages of these early Germanic invaders. The text opposite is taken from a German language magazine for learners.

Children can be asked to look at the pictures and the text opposite or, better still, hear someone with knowledge of German read it aloud. The following questions on the text are designed to get children to think about the links between English and German:

1) What is the text about?
2) How do you know this?
3) Are there any words in the German text that look or sound the same or nearly the same in English? *(Popcorn, Plastik, Minuten, Millionen, Pop, Name)*
4) Are there any other words which are a bit like English? (*Mais* = maize, *produziert* = produced, *explodiert* = explodes, *Pfanne* = pan, *Wasser* = water, *Tonnen* = tons, *Zucker* = sugar, *Salz* = salt, *Öl* = oil).

NICHT NUR POPCORN...

Popcorn ist eine tolle Erfindung, aber wer ist der geniale Erfinder? Eigentlich entsteht Popcorn aus Mais. Die Mayas waren das erste Volk, das Mais anbaute. Aber schon kurze Zeit später wurde auf der ganzen Welt Mais angepflanzt, weil er schnell wächst und wenig Pflege braucht.

Stellt euch einmal vor, heute werden weltweit jährlich 500 Millionen Tonnen produziert! Aber nicht nur Popcorn wird aus Mais hergestellt, sondern auch Medikamente, Zucker und sogar umweltfreundliches Plastik. In Zukunft werden alle Einkaufstüten aus Mais gemacht.

So wird Popcorn gemacht: (siehe Zeichnung)

Aber warum heißt es Popcorn?
In jedem Maiskorn steckt ein Wassertröpfchen. Dieses explodiert, wenn es erhitzt wird und macht dabei "Pop". Daher der Name "Popcorn".

Gib den Mais und etwas Öl in eine Pfanne.

Decke die Pfanne zu und stelle sie auf die Herdplatte.

Nach wenigen Minuten ist das Popcorn fertig. Mit etwas Salz schmeckt es köstlich.

Children could also discuss any other things they notice about German as a language, such as the use of capital letters for nouns, how German makes nouns plural, the umlaut over certain vowels which changes the sound. This kind of exercise helps children to develop language learning skills and strategies such as noticing patterns and structures or using cognates and non-verbal clues to aid comprehension.

The influence of Old Norse, another Germanic language, can also be seen in many English words. Many very ordinary words in English have derived from Old Norse. For example, 'husband' (Old Norse: *husbondi*), 'leg' (Old Norse: *leggr*), and 'skirt' (Old Norse: *skyrta* = shirt). Many English words beginning with 'sk' or 'sc' also have their origins in Old Norse. For example, 'skill' (Old Norse: *skil* = distinction), 'scare' (Old Norse: *skirra* = frighten). Children can be asked to think of or find in a dictionary words beginning with 'sk' and check to see if they originate in Old Norse. This language also greatly influenced the grammatical structure of simple sentences in present day English.

A further important influence on English came from French, following the Norman invasion of 1066. Because French is a 'Romance' language (deriving from Latin, the language of the Romans), it brought a different set of vocabulary into English. As the Norman invaders became the ruling classes, words associated with government, law, religion, the military and nobility tend to derive from French. Similarly, with the invasion of the Mughals into India in the 14th century, many Sanskrit words for law and order were replaced by Perso-Arabic words, such as *kanoon* (law), *muzrim* (accused), *adalat* (court), *tukht* (throne), as the invading force wanted to show authority and power. This shows the links between language and political power in the cultural histories of different countries.

As they are told the stories of these invasions, children could be asked to produce posters illustrating sets of vocabulary, for example English words from Anglo-Saxon/Old Norse/Norman French or Hindi words from the Persian language. After hearing the historical facts, they could role play or write a typical conversation in English, for example, between Anglo-Saxon farmers (using words derived from Anglo-Saxon or Old Norse), and Norman aristocrats (using words derived from Norman French).

Anglo-Saxon/Old Norse words	*Norman words*
Nouns	
shirt (Old Norse = *skyrta*)	castle (Old Northern French = *castel)*
egg (Old English/Old Saxon = œg)	rob (Old French *rober = to rob, plunder*)
husband (Old Norse = *husbondi*)	messenger (Old French = *messager*)
cow (Old English/Old Saxon = *cu*)	chamber (Old French = *chambre*)
window (Old Norse = *vindauga*)	letter (Old French = *lettre*)
Verbs	
eat (Old English/Old Saxon = *etan*)	imprison (Old French = *emprisoner*)
sit (Old English/Old Saxon = *sittian*)	deliver (Old French = *delivrer*)
help (Old English/Old Saxon = *help*)	enter (Old French = *entrer*)
fall (Old English/Old Saxon = *f(e)allen*)	aid (Old French = *aidier*)
Adjectives/adverbs	
slow/slowly (Old English/Old Saxon = *slaw*)	foolish/foolishly (Old French = *fol*)
hard (Old English/Old Saxon = *h(e)ard*)	gentle/gently (Old French = *gentil*)
thin (Old English/Old Saxon = *thynne*)	huge (Old French = *ahuge/aho(e)ge*)

OTHER DERIVATIONS

Over the centuries, English has continued to borrow words from many other languages and has evolved accordingly. As with the early invasions, most of these borrowings are attached to historical events and the stories behind word borrowings often help to open children's minds to other languages and cultures. The *Word story detective game* described below provides a way of showing children how words from many other languages are used in English.

WORD STORY DETECTIVE GAME

Each group of children works with a set of coloured cards containing individual words which have derived from other languages, for example:

As well as the word cards, the children are given cards in another colour containing the 'story' of each word derivation (see below). The game consists of matching the word with its 'story', as in a 'pairs' card game. All the cards are turned face down and each child in turn takes a word card and a 'story' card and reads them out aloud to see if they match – if so, the child keeps the cards. The idea is to get as many matching cards as possible.

The Turkish word *tulband* and the Persian word *dulband* mean a turban and describe the shape of this flower.

This word comes from the Japanese for 'great lord'. What does it mean in English?

When the Normans invaded England in 1066 they introduced many new ideas for defending territory such as stone towers, walls and battlements

This word comes from Hindi and relates to the huge chariot which is taken out in procession with great pomp and ceremony to carry an image of Jaggannath, 'lord of the universe'.

Originally from a Chinese dialect, this word travelled to Malaysia and then the Netherlands. It is a drink imported into England in the seventeenth century and has since become very popular.

This word is made up of two Latin words, one meaning 'air' and the other from the verb *solvere* meaning to release.

This vegetable gets its name from Spanish after Spanish explorers in South America enjoyed eating it. It was brought to England in the sixteenth century by Sir Walter Raleigh.

This word was the surname of an American manufacturer who made the original machine in the early twentieth century.

Teachers can find many examples of words to use for this sort of activity by looking in an etymological dictionary to find the source of words from a range of languages borrowed in English.

As well as other languages influencing English, English words have also been borrowed by other languages. When we hear speakers talking in an unfamiliar language we can often identify some English vocabulary, especially words connected with modern technology. These words have been fully assimilated into a number of languages, and have adapted to the phonetics of these languages. For example, the word 'station' or 'film' in English becomes *istition* and *filum* in some dialects of Hindi and other Indian languages. These words and many others have travelled to different parts of the world together with the technology of Western cultures. Often when an aspect of culture travels with a related word from one part of the world to another, the word then becomes assimilated into the host language. This can be clearly seen with the word 'pyjamas'. In its original context in India, it literally means leg-clothing or covering. It is usually a pair of drawstring loose trousers mainly made in fine white cotton for tropical wear. However, as the word travelled to England it adopted a new meaning befitting the climate and culture. Children who know other languages can give examples or ask their parents for examples and discuss why they think the word has been borrowed. When listening to a story told in another language (as suggested in Chapter 3), children can listen out for English words and put their hands up or stand up when they hear one. They can then discuss with the storyteller why the English word is used. For example, a mother getting her son Rajul out of bed in the morning, saying in Hindi "Rajul, utho utho, jaldi nahito, *train miss* Kerjaogey."

WORD-BUILDING

Many words in English and in other languages are compound words containing **prefixes**, **suffixes** or, in some languages such as Turkish, **infixes** (fitted into the middle of a word). English prefixes have often derived from Greek or Latin. The word television, for example, contains the Greek prefix *tele* meaning 'far' while 'vision' derives from the Latin *videre,* to see. Children can be asked to think of other words in English or other languages beginning with 'tele' and see if they can relate them to the meaning 'far'. The Greek word *photo* means 'light' and is again often attached to other word parts. Children could explain or do a drawing to show the original meanings of the word parts for 'photograph', 'photocopy', etc. The Latin prefix *super* (meaning over, above, extra) could be used to invent imaginative new words such as *supertrousers* or *superbird*. Children could have fun drawing

these new words and telling stories about them. In Hindi and many other Indian languages the prefix *su* (good) when added to the main word, for example, *ruchi* (taste) means 'good taste' while the opposite *ku* when added to *ruchi* means 'bad taste'. Teachers can ask children to identify the prefix in other Hindi words, for example *unoochit* (*oochit* means thoughtful or reasonable, *un*, just like English, implies the opposite). Children can collect and compare examples of prefixes in the languages they know. This will strengthen their understanding of compound words. Sometimes a story can stimulate a discussion about linguistic features such as prefixes. For example the story in Hindi about an unthoughtful man in the village *ek gaun ki ek unoochit aadmi ki kahani* (literally a village's unthoughtful man's story).

The suffix *wallah* used in many Indian languages denotes a person with a specific job and the accompanying rituals associated with it. The term has been absorbed into the English language since the 1960s following the well-known Ivory-Merchant film *Shakespearewallah*. This is the story of a devoted group of actors in India who travel around, sometimes with great difficulties, to stage Shakespeare's plays to the delight of their audiences who join in the rendition of Shakespeare's verses. Some Hindi suffixes, such as *-ji* are used to show respect and endearment to a person. In an Indian gathering one of the authors of this book was once addressed as *Cathy-ji* out of respect and affection.

CODE-SWITCHING

Many people, when they speak, bring in words from other languages. Most of the time this is done unconsciously and is influenced by the topic or the persons involved in the conversation. They switch between languages for a range of reasons, for example:

- to express something for which there is no equivalent English word, often words strongly associated with the culture (such as the suffix *-ji* mentioned above);

- to enrich the conversation in English;

- switching from the mother tongue to English to maintain fluency in a conversation depending on the context, theme or personal relationship;

- to express something about themselves and their original culture;

- to communicate friendship or solidarity.

This can be viewed negatively, especially by people who do not understand the underlying reasons or strengths of code-switching. It is particularly important for teachers to be attuned to code-switching by pupils and to approach it positively. In many classrooms with diverse languages it is often observed that children fluent in English interpret and repeat the teacher's instructions in another language (Bengali, Turkish, Somali, etc) for the speakers of these languages who are at an earlier stage of learning English.

Four year-old Ayse phones her grandmother every day after nursery and tells her about her day at the English-speaking nursery. For this she uses Kurdish and demonstrates her ability to recall and sequence the events of the day, describe them, share her emotions and answer her grandmother's questions. We see a range of rich linguistic and literacy skills being developed in this interaction. Ayse is transferring these skills from English to Kurdish and vice versa.

Code-switching indicates a developing fluency between languages. Nadia was a fluent storyteller in Bengali at five. As her English developed, the storytelling in Bengali absorbed many English words, especially nouns. For example when telling the story of the Monkey and the Crocodile (a traditional story from Bangladesh), she switched to English for words like 'crocodile', 'banana', 'monkey'. This did not interrupt the flow of her story which her bilingual friends enjoyed enormously.

The activity below is adapted from *The languages book* (ILEA English Centre 1981). It shows how code-switching activities can be organised which can help develop a positive attitude to switching languages.

Opposite are some phrases in the Creole language spoken by the people of St Lucia, a small Caribbean island. This language has borrowed a lot from French but has its own words and phrases and rules.

Bõʒu – Good morning, hello
Bõswè – Good evening
S'u Plè – Please
Padõn – Excuse me
Mwẽ Pèdi – I'm lost
Koté mwẽ – Where am I ?
Mwẽ so èk las – I'm hot and tired
Ès diné pàwé – Is dinner ready?
Mwẽ Ka-alé – I'm going; Goodbye
Mwẽ èmé u – I like you
Mwẽ pa èmé u – I don't like you
U ès fu! – You're crazy!

Children are asked to try and hold a conversation in St Lucian, with one person using these phrases and the other using mainly English, then swapping roles. The idea is to try to keep the conversation going as long as possible – just keep talking!

Even in schools where there are not many bilingual children, some of the principles explored in this chapter can be applied to working with different varieties of English.

Teachers can use poems or stories written in local dialect to initiate a discussion of how the use of the dialect contributes to the meaning of the text. Such a discussion raises the same points mentioned earlier in this chapter about the reasons for switching between languages.

The poem 'Micky always' is written in Jamaican English. This is a good poem to use for performance. A child with knowledge of Jamaican English can take the lead or an adult could be invited to 'perform' the poem with the class. Children could be asked to think how the rhythm and tone of Jamaican English adds to the life of the poem.

Micky always

Bambalitty-Bambam
Bambalitty-Bambam
Everybody scram, scram.
Micky hit the ball so hard
it gone right out the yard
and break the lady window-pane
He Micky don't hear, just don't hear.
Bambalitty-Bambam
Bambalitty-Bambam
Everybody scram, scram.
Micky break the lady window-pane
and when the lady come and complain
Mammy give him plai-plai
then you going to hear Micky cry.
I din do Nuttin

(John Agard 1983)

A discussion on this variety of English could follow with children discussing the similarities and differences compared to Standard English.

This chapter has shown how looking at the English language from a perspective of diversity can help children to understand how languages have always interrelated and evolved interdependently. This has become increasingly significant in the modern technological world. In a diverse society like Britain, this also helps children to transfer the skills and knowledge they have acquired in their first or home language to other language learning experiences. Children's awareness of the diverse history of the English language and of the links between English and many other languages can be supported by the activities described in this chapter. As well as deepening their understanding of how English works as a language (with its links to numerous other languages), these activities will help to raise children's curiosity about and interest in languages and will foster children's identities as language learners of the future.

Conclusion

In preparing this book we have talked to children who have shared with us their knowledge and understanding of language enthusiastically and energetically. This experience has been enormously rewarding for us. We believe that our teacher colleagues will enjoy using the interactive activities suggested in the book, for example, drama, games, singing, investigations, cooking, stories and rhymes. These are activities with which every primary teacher is familiar. What we are suggesting, however, is that these can also be carried out in other languages as well as in English. The outcomes can be very rewarding, allowing young children to share their insights into language and their metalinguistic understandings, thus enriching the language and literacy learning promoted by the National Curriculum and the National Literacy Strategy. The chapter on 'Managing multilingual activities' empowers all teachers to include parents and other adults in school and the community in order to achieve these goals. The activities in the book have been used by teachers, student teachers and children in a range of classrooms and their stories are testimony to the positive benefits of using multilingual approaches to language work in the primary classroom.

> *Britain is often recognised as a country with profoundly monolingual assumptions and a widespread apathy towards learning other languages.*

(Stubbs, in Garcia and Baker, 1995)

Acknowledging the community languages of Britain and bridging the separateness of community and Modern Foreign Languages in children's language learning and development has been the aim of this book throughout. Sharing children's language histories, knowledge and skills is empowering for every child, and creates the inspiration and motivation to learn a new language. When energised, young learners seek out different pathways to pursue this, as the children in this book have demonstrated. Teachers, teaching assistants and other adults in schools, parents, friends and members of different communities are partners in this process and make it possible for them to learn and enjoy language learning collectively and collaboratively.

References

Ben-Zeev, S. (1977) 'The influence of bilingualism on cognitive strategy and cognitive development'. In: *Child Development,* 48:1009–1018.

Bettelheim, B. (1976) *The uses of enchantment: The meaning and importance of fairy tales.* Penguin Books.

Chao, Y. R. (1968) *Language and symbolic systems.* Cambridge University Press.

Cheater, C. and Farren, A. (2001) Young Pathfinder 9: *The literacy link.* CILT.

Cummins, J. (1996) *Negotiating identities: Education for empowerment in a diverse society.* Ontario: CABE.

Datta, M. (2000) *Bilinguality and literacy: Principles and practice.* Continuum.

Edwards, V. (1998) *The power of Babel: Teaching and learning in multilingual classrooms.* Trentham Books.

European Language Portfolio – junior version (2001). CILT.

Fishman, J.A. (1991) *Reversing language shift.* Multilingual Matters.

Garcia, O. and Baker, C. (1995) *Policy and practice in bilingual education.* Multilingual Matters.

Gumperz, J. J. (1982) *Discourse strategies.* Cambridge University Press.

Hester, H. (1983) *Stories in the multilingual primary classroom.* London ILEA.

Hrubin, F. :(1953) 'Sluníèko Sedmiteèné'. In: František Hrubín and Zábranský, A. (1953) *Je nám dobøe na svìtì.* Prague: Státní nakladatelství dìtské knihy.

Johnstone, R. (1993) 'Research on language and teaching: 1992' *Language Teaching, 26*: 131–43.

Katzner, K. (2002) *The languages of the world.* Routledge.

Klein-Smith, S. (1994) 'It felt like being a baby all over again'. In: *The voice inside.* Hackney Education and Leisure.

Krashen, S. (1982) *Principles and practices of second language acquisition.* Pergamon Press.

Lawrence, D. (1999) *Inclusive schools, inclusive society: Race and identity on the agenda* (Foreword). Trentham Books.

Martin, C. and Cheater, C. (1998) Young Pathfinder 6: *Let's join in: Rhymes, poems and songs*. CILT.

National Oracy Project. (1990) *Teaching talking and learning in Key Stage 1*. National Curriculum Council.

Room, A. (1988) *Dictionary of place names in the British Isles*. Bloomsbury Publishing.

Schumann, J. (1978) *The pidginization process: A model for second language acquisition*. Rowley, MA: Newbury House.

Spolsky, B. (1989) *Conditions for second language learning*. Oxford University Press.

The languages book (1981). ILEA English Centre.

CHILDREN'S FICTION BOOKS

'The boogey man's wife'. In: Aardema, V. and Ruffins, R. (1995) *Misoso once upon a time tales from Africa*. Hamish Hamilton.

Agard, J. 'Micky always' from Agard, J. (1983) *I din do nuttin and other poems*. Bodley Head.

Browne, E. (1994) *Handa's surprise*. Walker Books.

Burningham, J. (1970) *Mr Gumpy's outing*. Cape.

Gray, N. and Ray, J. (1988) *A balloon for Grandad*. Orchard Picturebooks.

Kessler, C. and Schoenherr, I. (1996) *Muhamed's desert night*. Puffin Books.

Rosen, M. and Oxenbury, H. (1989) *We're going on a bear hunt*. Walker Books.

Waddell, M. and Oxenbury, H. (1993) *Farmer duck* (Vietnamese/English dual-language version). Magi Publications.

Government plans for an entitlement to early language learning pose an exciting challenge for all primary schools. CILT can help you to deliver that entitlement in your school.

NACELL (the National Advisory Centre on Early Language Learning), established at CILT and on-line, offers you support through information on:

- what's happening in schools
- teaching resources, including CILT publications
- training courses
- joining the ell-forum
- ELL Regional Support Groups
- publications, including the CILT *ELL Bulletin*
- the *European Language Portfolio – Junior version*
- the *NACELL best practice guide*

Find out also about **CILT Direct Primary**, the membership scheme which provides enhanced access to the above, through regular mailings and discounts on conferences and publications.

Membership enquiries tel: 020 7379 5101 ext. 232. Information is also available on the NACELL website

A number of LEAs are using the European Language Portfolio extensively – finding it a valuable tool in the critical transition stage to Secondary

COUNCIL   CONSEIL
OF EUROPE   DE L'EUROPE
European Language Portfolio
Portfolio européen des langues

European Language Portfolio – Junior version

The *European Language Portfolio* is:
* a means of celebrating language-learning experiences;
* an open-ended record of children's achievements in languages;
* a valuable source of information to aid transfer to the next class or school.

It consists of:
* **Language passport** – providing an overview of the learner's knowledge and experiences of different languages, including cultural experiences;
* **Language biography** – a personalised learning diary making children aware of their achievements;
* **Getting better!** – an opportunity for learner self-assessment which can be used to encourage children to reflect on their progress;
* **Dossier** – offering learners the opportunity to select work and materials to illustrate the achievements recorded elsewhere in the Portfolio.

The Portfolio is addressed to and is the property of the learner. An accompanying *Teacher's Guide* is also available.

The European Language Portfolio is a Council of Europe initiative being implemented for learners at all stages of education across Europe. The UK's Junior European Language Portfolio was approved for use in 2001.

RESOURCE *file*

Pathfinder support materials
for language teachers

ResourceFiles provide a wealth of innovative ideas and ready-to-use *photocopiable* classroom activities, helping teachers to develop their teaching approaches and add variety to their lessons. All materials are supported by detailed teacher's notes.

Getting the basics right (RF3)
Nouns, gender and adjectives
Lydia Biriotti

Rhythm and rhyme (RF6)
Developing language in French and German
Cynthia Martin

See **www.cilt.org.uk** for further details of all CILT publications